The
Homeless

The
Homeless

Christopher
Jencks

Harvard University Press
Cambridge, Massachusetts
London, England
1994

SECOND PRINTING, 1994

This book is printed on acid-free paper.

Library of Congress Cataloging-in-Publication Data
Jencks, Christopher.
The homeless / Christopher Jencks.
p.   cm.
Includes bibliographical references.
ISBN 0-674-40595-1
1. Homelessness—United States.
2. Homelessness—Government
policy—United States.
HV4505.J46   1994
362.5′8′0973—dc20
93-46424
CIP

Preface

Late in the 1970s Americans began noticing more people sleeping in public places, wandering the streets with their possessions in shopping bags, rooting through garbage bins in search of food or cans, and asking for handouts. By January 1981, when Ronald Reagan took office, a small group of activists led by Robert Hayes and Mitch Snyder had given these people a new name—"the homeless"—and had begun to convince politicians and journalists that homelessness was a serious problem.

Later that year America entered its worst recession in half a century, and the homeless became far more visible. Most Americans initially saw this as a temporary problem that would vanish once the economy recovered, but they turned out to be wrong. Unemployment fell from almost 10 percent in 1983 to just over 5 percent in 1989, but homelessness kept rising.

The spread of homelessness disturbed affluent Americans for both personal and political reasons. At a personal level, the faces of the homeless often suggest depths of despair that we would rather not imagine, much less confront in the flesh. Daily contact with the homeless also raises troubling and ultimately unanswerable questions about our moral obligations to strangers. At a political level, the spread of homelessness suggests that something has gone fundamentally wrong with America's economic or social institutions.

Because homelessness is both heart-wrenching and politically controversial, it has inspired a steady flow of books and reports by journalists, political activists, and scholars. This essay began as a review of such books. In 1989 Robert Silvers of the *New York Review of Books* asked me to review Peter Rossi's *Down and Out in America*. I agreed, but I also procrastinated. Silvers retaliated by sending me more books on the subject. My shelves began to fill. In due course my review grew into an essay discussing eight books and two reports.

Because other writers have described the lives of the homeless far better than I can, this book tells no stories about individuals. Instead, I try to answer three historical and political questions. How much did homelessness increase during the 1980s? Why did it increase? And what should we now do to reduce it?

I begin by discussing various ways of counting the homeless and estimating the increase in homelessness between 1980 and 1990. Next I look at the social and political changes that I think contributed most to the spread of homelessness: the virtual abolition of involuntary commitment for the mentally ill, failure to provide alternative housing for many of those we deinstitutionalized, the crack epidemic, increased long-term joblessness among working-age men, the declining frequency of marriage among women with children, reductions in cash welfare benefits, and the destruction of skid row. After that I examine some changes to which I assign minor roles: families' growing reluctance to shelter their down-at-heel kin, changes in the private housing market, cutbacks in federal spending for low-income housing, and local rent-control ordinances. Finally, I discuss whether opening shelters has encouraged more people to become homeless and propose some possible strategies for reducing the problem in the years ahead.

Acknowledgments

This is the first book I have written without a coauthor, but that does not mean I wrote it on my own. I owe an immense debt to David Rhodes, who spent hundreds of hours at his computer terminal analyzing Census surveys. He produced most of the numbers that appear in my text and tables. Without his patience and expertise I would never have been able to write a book of this kind. Judith Levine played an equally crucial role in helping me analyze the Labor Department's Consumer Expenditure Survey. Tim Veenstra made and remade the graphs.

I also owe more than I can say to the authors whose books prodded me to write one of my own: Martha Burt *(Over the Edge)*, Charles Hoch and Robert Slayton *(New Homeless and Old)*, Elliot Liebow *(Tell Them Who I Am)*, Peter Rossi *(Down and Out in America)*, David Snow and Leon Anderson *(Down on Their Luck)*, Jennifer Toth *(The Mole People)*, William Tucker *(The Excluded Americans)*, and Richard White *(Rude Awakenings)*. Although I disagree with some of their conclusions, and they will surely disagree with many of mine, they taught me most of what I have learned about homelessness. Michael Aronson at Harvard University Press was instrumental in persuading me to turn my original review essay into a book.

Many journalists, political activists, foundation executives, civil servants, and social scientists critiqued early drafts of this book. They included Barry Bearak, Rebecca Blank, Cushing Dolbeare, Mark Elliott, Herbert Gans, Irwin Garfinkel, Naomi Gerstel, Nathan Glazer, Howard

Goldman, Robert Greenstein, Kim Hopper, Stephen Jencks, Edward Lazere, Bruce Link, Jane Mansbridge, Susan Mayer, William McAllister, Brendan O'Flaherty, Kathryn Nelson, Peter Rossi, Michael Schwartz, Robert Silvers, David Whitman, Christopher Winship, and Barbara Wolfe. I am also indebted to all those who participated in a day-long discussion of the manuscript at the Russell Sage Foundation in October 1993, and to those who commented on earlier public presentations at Northwestern University and the University of Chicago. Some of these individuals agreed with my arguments, while others were highly critical. Together they saved me from more errors than I care to recall.

I have also received unusually generous institutional support while working on this and related issues. The Center for Urban Affairs and Policy Research at Northwestern University has given me stimulating colleagues, research assistants, and time off from teaching since 1979, despite the fact that all my projects, including this one, took at least twice as long as I promised. A grant from the Rockefeller Foundation to the Social Science Research Council's Committee on the Urban Underclass, of which I was at one time a member, paid for some of David Rhodes's time.

Finally, the Russell Sage Foundation allowed me to spend ten blissful months as a visiting scholar at its headquarters in New York City during 1991–92. Living in New York gave me a new perspective on homelessness, and working at the foundation gave me time to start writing. Throughout that year the president of the foundation, Eric Wanner, provided both moral support and thoughtful suggestions. He also displayed exemplary self-restraint when he discovered that my work on homelessness would further delay the long overdue book I had promised to complete during my year at the foundation.

I doubt that I will ever be able to repay all of these debts, but acknowledging them is a small step toward setting the balance right.

Contents

The
Homeless

1. Counting the Homeless

As soon as homelessness became a political issue, legislators and journalists began asking for numbers. The Census Bureau was in no position to answer their questions because it had always counted the population by making lists of "dwelling units" and then trying to determine how many people lived in each unit. The Bureau had never made much effort to count people living in bus stations, subways, abandoned buildings, doorways, or dumpsters. Nor did it try to fill this gap when public interest in the homeless exploded in the early 1980s. Even the 1990 Census, which tried to conduct a systematic count of people in shelters for the homeless, made only a half-hearted effort to count homeless people who were not in shelters.[1]

Numbers as Political Rhetoric

In the absence of official statistics, both journalists and legislators turned to advocacy groups. In the late 1970s Mitch Snyder had argued that a million Americans were homeless. In 1982 he and Mary Ellen Hombs raised their estimate to between two and three million.[2] Lacking better figures, journalists, legislators, and advocates for the homeless repeated this guess, usually without attribution. In due course it became so familiar that many people treated it as an established fact.

Widespread acceptance of Snyder's estimate apparently convinced the Reagan Administration that leaving statistics on homelessness to private enterprise was a political mistake, and in 1984 the Department of Housing and Urban Development (HUD) produced some numbers of its own. HUD telephoned the most knowledgeable informants it could find in each large American city and asked them to estimate the number of homeless people in their metropolitan area. The Department's analysts then picked a number near the middle of the range for each area. Extrapolating from these estimates, HUD's best estimate of the homeless population in the nation as a whole was between 250,000 and 350,000.[3]

This new estimate was so much lower than Snyder's that many people assumed HUD must have fiddled the data. But when Ted Koppel asked Snyder on *Nightline* where his own estimate of two to three million homeless had come from, this is what Snyder said:

> Everybody demanded it. Everybody said we want a number . . . We got on the phone, we made a lot of calls, we talked to a lot of people, and we said, "Okay, here are some numbers." They have no meaning, no value.[4]

But while Snyder conceded that his own numbers had no value, he nonetheless denounced HUD's numbers as "tripe." He did not fault HUD's methods, which were much like those he himself apparently used. He simply rejected HUD's conclusions. If HUD's numbers were accepted, he told Koppel, they would "take some of the power away . . . some of our potential impact . . . and some of the resources we might have access to, because we're not talking about something that's measured in millions."[5]

Snyder was right. If you want to hold the attention of the mass media, breaking the "million barrier" is important. This is why many advocates for the homeless still tell reporters and funders that several million Americans are homeless, even though no careful study has ever yielded an estimate that high.[6] Many reporters who cover the homeless also continue to cite estimates above a million, partly because these estimates bolster their claim to prime time or front-page space.

Richard White, the author of *Rude Awakenings,* describes the repetition of these inflated estimates as "lying for justice." But that characterization, while memorable, implies that Snyder knew the true number was less than a million and exaggerated in a conscious effort to mislead the public. In reality, Snyder had no idea how many people were homeless. When he cited a figure between two and three million, he just meant "this is a big problem." Likewise, when he dismissed HUD's lower estimate as tripe, he just meant "they say it's a small problem, but I say it's a big one."

In debates of this kind one needs to distinguish between scientific and political numbers. This distinction has nothing to do with accuracy. Scientific numbers are often wrong, and political numbers are often right. But scientific numbers are accompanied by enough documentation so you can tell who counted what, whereas political numbers are not. Right or wrong, HUD's 1984 numbers were reasonably well documented, while Snyder's earlier numbers were not.

What Is a Home?

Anyone who really wants to know how many people are homeless has to start by deciding what to count as a home. Many Americans still use the term "home" as a synonym for the place where their family lives. People without family ties are then "homeless" no matter where they live. Building on this conception, American sociologists used to describe men who lived in skid-row hotels as homeless. The label was not based on the fact that these hotels were overcrowded or badly ventilated. Sociologists called these men homeless because they lived alone and seldom saw their kin.

After 1960, as more and more Americans began living alone by choice, the idea that you had a home only if you lived with your family began to lose its grip on the American imagination. By the late 1960s many Americans thought they had a home if they had a fixed address where they could leave their possessions, return whenever they wished, and sleep in peace. The homeless were in turn defined as people who had no fixed address. Some were the occupational heirs of the old hobos, who were homeless because they did seasonal work that kept them constantly on the move. The rest were commonly known as "bums"—people who lived in the same community for long periods but had no regular work and were too poor or too disorganized to rent a room on a long-term basis.

Since 1980 most Americans have adopted an even less demanding view of what it means to have a home. When we talk about the homeless today, we seldom include migrant workers. Today any private space intended for sleeping can qualify as a home, so long as those who sleep in it have a legal right to be there and can exclude strangers. The homeless have become those who have no private space of their own, however temporary.

On any given night, the homeless can be divided into two groups: those who sleep in free shelters (the "shelter homeless") and those who sleep in places not intended for human habitation, such as bus stations, subway trains, automobiles, doorways, and abandoned buildings. Those who sleep outside shelters are generally known as the "street homeless," even though many sleep in abandoned buildings, bus stations, and other indoor locations. The distinction between the street and shelter homeless works fairly well on any given night, but it breaks down when we follow people over time. Only a minority of the homeless report having spent all of the past seven nights in the same place.[7] Many report that they were in a shelter one night, a subway station the next, and a friend's home the night after that.

Everyone seems to agree that people who sleep regularly in bus stations, abandoned buildings, doorways, and other places "not intended for sleeping" are homeless. But people are supposed to sleep in shelters. That makes the line between a shelter and a home harder to draw. Everyone agrees that single adults who sleep alongside strangers in a barrack-like shelter do not have a home. That is doubly true if, as is usually the case, they do not have access to this space during the day. But families living in what have come to be called welfare hotels pose more difficult questions.

Welfare hotels (or sometimes motels) are places to which local welfare departments send families with children when they have no shelter space available. Each family usually has its own room and, in most cases, its own bathroom. The rooms are obviously crowded, but they meet the privacy test, and families have access to them whenever they want. If a family in a welfare hotel paid its own rent, we would never call it homeless. In recent years, however, almost everyone who has counted the homeless has included families in welfare hotels.

Although families in welfare hotels do not pay their own rent, that fact alone is not sufficient to explain why we label them homeless. Millions of American families live in federally subsidized housing, often paying only token rent, yet nobody calls them homeless. What, then, is the difference between a welfare hotel and either a public housing project or a private apartment for which the federal government pays most of the rent?

A welfare hotel is supposed to be a temporary way station on the road to something better. America has no law preventing families from living in one-room apartments or guaranteeing them something more spacious. But we do, in effect, guarantee those families fortunate enough to get government subsidies something better, at least in the long run. The government cannot put families in one room indefinitely without becoming embroiled in political and legal controversies that most politicians desperately want to avoid. So when the government puts families in a single room, everyone has an interest in claiming that the situation is temporary.

Another crucial difference between a welfare hotel and other kinds of subsidized housing is that welfare hotels are paid for by a government agency that is not supposed to be in the housing business. If state legislatures set welfare benefits high enough so that recipients could afford unsubsidized housing, no family with children would have to stay in a welfare hotel for more than a few days. At present, however, welfare recipients can seldom afford unsubsidized housing unless they have additional unreported income, over and above what they get from welfare.[8] If they do not have such income, they need some kind of housing subsidy. Since there is not enough subsidized housing for everyone who is legally eligible, welfare departments are always looking for a way of getting their clients to the head of the waiting list. Calling a family homeless is a way of helping it jump the queue.

Advocates for the homeless endorse this expansive definition of homelessness. They assume that families in welfare hotels and shelters need a subsidized apartment more than the other families on the waiting list, even if the other families have been waiting longer. In most cases that is true, since a family's willingness to move into a welfare hotel is a measure of its desperation. Advocates also want to count families in welfare hotels as homeless because they want to raise the overall count and include more children, who evoke more public sympathy than homeless adults.

Many housing activists also argue that homeless counts should include people who are doubled up in someone else's home. Many ordinary Americans certainly use the term this way. In 1990, for example, a telephone survey conducted by Bruce Link and his colleagues asked American adults, "Have you ever had a time in your life when you considered yourself homeless?" Fifteen percent of adults said they had been homeless at some point in their lives, but only 9 percent had ever lived in a shelter or on the streets.[9] The rest had been doubled up.

In order to count the doubled-up homeless, however, we would need to distinguish between voluntary and involuntary doubling up. We would also need to know whether people who are doubled up have private space of their own. Ideally, the Census Bureau should ask adults whether their name is on the title or lease to their home, whether they are paying rent to the owner or primary tenant, whether they have a room of their own, whether they would like to get a place of their own, and so on. But the Bureau has never done this, and neither has anyone else. At present, therefore, statistics on people who are doubled up include not only those who have no money and nowhere else to go but rich widows who live with their children by choice, young adults who live with their parents so they can save money for a new car, unmarried lovers who live together for romantic reasons, and roommates who live together because they would otherwise be lonely. Counting all these people as homeless—or even as having a housing problem—would make no sense.

Few Americans worry much about people who live with relatives or friends, even if they are sleeping on the living-room floor. In some cases, however, the line separating those who are doubled up from those who are literally homeless is as permeable as the line separating the shelter homeless from the street homeless. Although some homeless adults have not slept in conventional housing for years, others move back and forth between conventional housing, shelters, and the streets on an almost daily basis. Peter Rossi's 1985–86 survey of the Chicago homeless found that a third of those who were sleeping in a shelter or a public place on any given night had spent at least one night during the previous week in someone else's home or in a hotel.[10] These people may have slept more soundly on the nights they spent in conventional housing, but they can hardly be said to have had a home on those nights.

A logically consistent approach to counting the homeless would probably require us to adopt either a physical standard or a subjective standard. If we wanted to define homelessness in physical terms, we could classify individuals and families as homeless if they had no private space of their own to which they had continuous access. By that standard, families in welfare hotels would have a home, but some families and individuals who are currently doubled up would not. If we wanted to define homelessness in more subjective terms, we could classify adults as homeless if they did not have a place of their own, said they wanted one, and said money was the primary obstacle to getting one. Using a subjective rather than a physical standard would not make families in welfare hotels homeless, but it would make us count more people who are currently doubled up as homeless.

In this book I define homelessness more narrowly, concentrating on the people whose existence most worries the public. I include everyone who slept in a public place or a shelter during a given week, and I treat welfare hotels as a species of shelter. I ignore people who are in jails, detoxification centers, mental hospitals, or other institutions throughout the week, despite the fact that many of them come from the streets and will return to the streets as soon as they are released. I include children in family shelters and welfare hotels, but I ignore both teenage runaways and children in foster care, many of whom are far more homeless than most children in shelters.

This list should serve as a reminder, if any is needed, that what I am really writing about is what we might call the "visible homeless"— people whose presence on the streets upsets the more prosperous classes. These are not necessarily the poorest or the most deprived of our fellow citizens. If we look in jails, detox centers, mental hospitals, and foster homes, we can find hundreds of thousands of other Americans surviving without the physical or emotional support we normally associate with having a home. We do not count these people as homeless because they are out of sight. When people contemplate human misery, the cliché that equates "out of sight" with "out of mind" is all too accurate.

2. Estimating the Increase

The United States has never made a systematic national effort to count the homeless outside shelters. The only way to estimate the overall size of the homeless population is therefore to combine national shelter counts with various kinds of local data on the frequency with which homeless families and individuals use shelters.

In March 1980, the Census Bureau counted 23,000 people sleeping in what were then called missions (a term derived from the fact that shelters had traditionally been run by evangelists who hoped to save lost souls). This count excluded an unknown number of shelter residents who failed to fill out their Census form or reported that they had a permanent address elsewhere. If all these people had been included, my best guess is that the 1980 count would have been around 35,000. (The rationale for this judgment is set forth in Appendix 1.)

Early in 1984, when HUD asked a sample of shelter managers how many people they had accommodated on an average January night, the estimated total was 70,000. By September 1988, when HUD did its next survey, managers' reports suggested that the system had housed an average of 180,000 people nightly during the previous year.[1]

In March 1990, the Census Bureau counted 190,000 people in shelters and very cheap hotels.[2] Roughly 10,000 of these individuals were in runaway shelters, which HUD did not cover, and something like 10,000 were probably in cheap hotels. The 1990 shelter count was therefore slightly lower than HUD's 1987–88 estimate. The shelter count may have risen since 1990 because of the recession, but there is no way of verifying this conjecture, because HUD's shelter surveys have been a victim of fiscal austerity. Unless HUD's plans change, we will not get another shelter count until the year 2000.

These estimates suggest that the nation's shelter population rose by a factor of roughly five between 1980 and 1990.[3] But this does not tell us how much the overall homeless population grew. In order to answer that question we need to know what proportion of the homeless used shelters in different years.

Counting the Unsheltered Homeless

Social scientists have tried to estimate what they call the "street-to-shelter" ratio in two ways. The most direct approach is to search public places in the small hours of the morning, identify everyone who has no home elsewhere, and compare the number of people found in public places to the number in shelters. A number of local surveys have tried to do this over the past decade. These surveys vary dramatically in quality, but even the best of them suffer from a serious problem. Those who spend the night in public places are often robbed or assaulted while they sleep, and in winter they also run the risk of freezing. Many therefore try to conceal themselves, preferably indoors. The more successful their efforts, the harder they are to count.

Manhattan, to take an extreme instance, is honeycombed with underground tunnels, most of which were built in the nineteenth century either for the subway system or to bring railroads into the city. Many of these tunnels are no longer used, but most can still be reached from above ground. Jennifer Toth, an intrepid young journalist who spent 1990 and 1991 exploring the New York tunnels with a diverse and terrifying variety of guides, concluded that at least 5000 people lived in them. An outreach program funded by the Metropolitan Transit Authority in 1990 claimed that over 6000 people were living in the tunnels around Grand Central and Penn Stations alone.[4] None of these people would show up in an early morning street count.

Finding people who sleep in abandoned buildings and automobiles poses similar problems. Interviewers are understandably reluctant to enter abandoned buildings, especially when the building is controlled by drug dealers. Yet a large fraction of the homeless use drugs, and these are precisely the buildings in which they are most likely to be found. People who sleep in automobiles and trucks also make an effort to park them where they will not be noticed. As a result, even the best early morning street count is likely to miss a significant fraction of the homeless.

A better way of counting the homeless, at least in my judgment, is to look for them during the day, when they make less effort to conceal themselves. Even the unsheltered homeless often use soup kitchens, where the food is free, the rules are few, and the dangers are limited. A large fraction of the homeless also frequent well-known congregating sites (train and bus stations, parks, particular streetcorners) where they can meet acquaintances, exchange news, pass the time, share a bottle, or buy drugs. Not all the homeless can be found in such places, but even Toth's tunnel residents often came up during the day to get food, hustle for money, and buy necessities. If one surveys the homeless during the day and asks where they spent the previous night, one can get a reasonable idea of how often they sleep in shelters. Since the number of shelter users is known with some accuracy, one can then estimate the overall size of the homeless population.

The most comprehensive survey of this kind was conducted by Martha Burt of the Urban Institute in March 1987. Burt surveyed a representative sample of large cities (those with more than 100,000 residents), interviewing randomly selected adults in three locations: shelters, soup kitchens, and congregating sites. Interviewers offered prospective respondents $5 for their time. As a result, over 90 percent of those approached agreed to an interview.[5]

Burt defined people as homeless if they met any of three tests:

(1) They said they had no home or permanent place to live.
(2) They said their home was a shelter, a hotel paid for with vouchers for the homeless, or a place not intended for sleeping.
(3) They said they lived in someone else's home but did not have a regular arrangement allowing them to stay there at least five days a week.[6]

All but 4 percent of the adults who met one of these tests had also spent at least one of the past seven nights in a shelter or a public place.[7] Burt's

Table 1. Characteristics of Homeless Persons in Cities of 100,000 or More, 1987

Family type and age	Percent
FAMILIES WITH CHILDREN	18.1
Children	12.2
Married parents	.8
Single parents	5.1
CHILDLESS GROUPS	8.1
Married couples	2.2
Unmarried but accompanied	5.9
ALONE	73.8
TOTAL	100.0
PERCENT IN SHELTERS ON AVERAGE NIGHT	
Families with children	95.8
Adults without children	34.3

Source: Urban Institute surveys directed by Martha Burt. Estimates exclude persons staying in other people's homes throughout the week before the interview and assume that rates of service use among the homeless adults in congregating sites are the same as for other homeless adults. Appendix 1 describes the derivation in detail.

definition of homelessness therefore coincides reasonably well with my preferred definition.

Table 1 provides a thumbnail sketch of the big-city homeless in 1987. Families with children accounted for only 18 percent of the homeless. Most of these families were headed by single mothers. Two-parent families were extremely rare. Intact marriages were also rare among those without children: only 3 percent of the homeless were accompanied by a spouse. Another 9 percent were accompanied by some other adult, who was sometimes a lover and sometimes a buddy. That left almost three quarters of the homeless completely alone.

I have also used Burt's data to estimate the fraction of the big-city homeless who used shelters on an average night. These estimates exclude people who said they were homeless but who had spent the entire week in someone else's home. They are shown separately for families with children and single adults. (Readers should be warned that in this book, as in most discussions of the homeless, the term "family" refers only to families with children, while the term "single" refers to the absence of children rather than the absence of a spouse.)

Table 1 shows that 96 percent of homeless families had spent the night before the interview in a shelter or a hotel paid for with vouchers.

Not a single family in Burt's sample said it had spent the previous night in a public building, an abandoned building, or outdoors.[8] Families that were not in shelters were either in someone else's home or in an automobile.

Burt's surveys undoubtedly missed a few homeless families. When Toth explored the New York tunnel system, she met a few children who did not even use soup kitchens much less sleep in shelters. But no one who has studied homeless families with children believes that many of them live in public places for long. The reason is simple: once the local authorities become aware of such families, they routinely take the children away from their parents and put them in foster care. Almost all homeless parents want to minimize the risk of losing their children, so they either send their children to live with relatives or move to a shelter.

Single adults have more choice about their living arrangements, although these choices are all pretty grim. My best guess, based on Burt's surveys, is that 34 percent of single adults slept in shelters on an average night in March 1987. Four percent slept in someone else's home or in a hotel they paid for with their own money. Most of the others passed the night in public places. Of these, the largest number were outdoors—in parks, on the streets, in doorways, and so on. Abandoned buildings were a close second, with public buildings third. A few had just been released from a jail, hospital, or detox center. Needless to say, sleeping patterns varied with the climate. In Chicago, hardly anyone sleeps out during March. In Los Angeles, many do.

Burt's survey provides quite a good picture of the visible homeless. It does not tell us much about those who avoid shelters, soup kitchens, and the company of other homeless individuals. I doubt that such people are numerous, but I can see no way of proving this. It is hard enough finding the proverbial needle in a haystack. It is far harder to prove that a haystack contains no more needles.

Table 1 portrays the big-city homeless. Rates of shelter use among the homeless in smaller cities seem to be similar. The street-to-shelter ratio in suburban Orange County during 1985 was similar to that in Alameda County, which includes Oakland. Seven years later, the street-to-shelter ratio in the Maryland and Virginia suburbs of Washington D.C. was also similar to that in the city itself. In Yolo County, California, which is extremely rural, the unsheltered homeless outnumbered the sheltered homeless by ten to one, but the total homeless population was very small.[9] Such evidence suggests that the rate of shelter use is about the same in smaller communities as in big cities.

Combining Burt's data on shelter use with national data on the size of the shelter population, my best guess is that about 350,000 Americans were homeless during March 1987.[10] That figure clearly has a large margin of error. Any figure between 300,000 and 400,000 would be easy to defend. Estimates above 500,000 are considerably harder to reconcile with the available evidence unless one believes that the "invisible" homeless are very numerous indeed.[11]

Turnover

Up to this point I have been trying to estimate the number of people who were homeless during a given week. We also need to ask how many of the people in conventional housing become homeless every week, and how many move back to conventional housing. The best data, I think, come from Link's 1990 survey of adults in conventional households. When asked about their experiences with homelessness, 3.1 percent said they had lived either in a shelter or on the streets within the past five years. That means roughly 1.2 million adults became homeless every year during the late 1980s. The number leaving the streets each year was almost equally high.[12]

Link's data suggest that half the adults who became homeless during the late 1980s were off the streets within a couple of months. Only one in eight remained homeless for more than a year. Nonetheless, half the people who are homeless on any given night will be homeless for more than a year.[13]

A simplified example may help explain this apparent paradox. Suppose a shelter has 40 beds that are always full. Ten are filled by a succession of individuals who remain homeless for exactly a week. Thirty are filled by people who remain homeless for a year. Over the course of a year, 520 people will enter the shelter and stay for a week while 30 enter and stay for a year. The shelter can now describe its clientele in two very different ways. If it wants to make its clients sound "normal," it can say that 95 percent of those who enter the shelter return to conventional housing within a week. If it wants to argue that its clients need all kinds of social services, it can say that 75 percent of its resources are devoted to people who remain homeless for a year.

The distinction between the short-term and the long-term homeless is important because they have somewhat different characteristics. Every attribute that raises an individual's chance of becoming homeless—limited job skills, weak family ties, mental illness, alcoholism, drug addiction, black skin, or having a Y chromosome, to name a few—also lowers an individual's chances of getting back into conventional housing. The long-term homeless therefore look even less like the general population than the short-term homeless do. Because the long-term homeless constitute the bulk of the homeless population on any given day, they dominate our perceptions of the homeless in general. They also consume the bulk of the public resources devoted to the homeless and experience most of the misery that afflicts the homeless.

Trends during the 1980s

We have no good national data on the number of people outside shelters before 1987. Indeed, Richard White argues that the total number of homeless persons may not have increased at all. He suspects that the "crisis" was created largely by advocates like Snyder and Hayes, who persuaded liberal journalists eager to discredit the Reagan Administration that an age-old problem was out of control.

At first I was tempted to dismiss this theory as ridiculous, on the grounds that the streets looked completely different in the late 1980s than in the late 1970s. But appearances can be deceptive, especially when we have to reconstruct them from memories going back well over a decade. There is no easy way of knowing whether a disheveled woman who sits talking to herself on a park bench is homeless. She could be homeless, but she could be living in a rooming house and getting federal disability benefits. Nor is there any way of knowing whether the panhandler working the subway is homeless. He certainly says he is, but he would say that even if he were living with his girlfriend and hustling for drug money.

Faced with an ambiguous situation, most of us reshape both our current impressions and our memories to make them consistent with our overall view of the world. In the late 1980s most Americans assumed that everyone on the streets who looked unkempt or confused was homeless. In the late 1970s, we assumed such people had a home unless we saw clear evidence to the contrary, such as a grocery cart full of personal possessions. These assumptions play a big role in determining what we remember.

But appearances can mislead us in the opposite way as well. When Rossi surveyed the Chicago homeless, his interviewers classified 55 percent of the people they interviewed as "neat and clean" rather than "dirty," "unkempt," or "shabbily dressed."[14] The neat and clean homeless sometimes betray their status by carrying their worldly goods in shopping bags, but they usually blend into the urban landscape unnoticed. Some even go to work every day, assiduously concealing their status from their employer and fellow workers.

Fortunately, we do not have to rely entirely on visual impressions to assess trends in homelessness. We also have earlier shelter counts. Since the shelter count rose by a factor of roughly five between 1980 and 1990, anyone who wants to argue that the homeless population remained constant has to argue that the rate of shelter use quintupled. While the proportion of the homeless using shelters rose during the 1980s, I doubt that it rose by anything like a factor of five.

The proportion of the homeless using shelters rose for several reasons. To begin with, we opened something like 3500 new shelters between 1984 and 1988.[15] Many of these new shelters were in communities that had never had a shelter before. In addition, some shelters relaxed their rules about how long residents could stay, and some upgraded their facilities. These changes were meant to pull the homeless in off the streets, and in some measure they succeeded.

The frequency with which the homeless use shelters also depends on what the alternatives are like. If single men who sleep in the park are set on fire by teenage gangs, robbed by drug users, or routinely arrested by the police, demand for shelter beds will be high. If the victimization rate is low and the police let the homeless sleep in certain parks or subway stations, demand for shelter beds will be lower. In some cases the police may even turn a public space into a semiofficial shelter. In Chicago, for example, there was a time during the 1980s when the police let hundreds of homeless individuals sleep in the international terminal at O'Hare Airport after the last plane had left. That presumably lowered demand for beds in conventional shelters. When the police reversed this policy, demand for conventional shelter beds presumably rose.

Much the same thing happened in many other cities during the 1980s. When public sympathy for the homeless was high and liberals controlled the city government, the police sometimes allowed the homeless to create encampments in public parks or other unused spaces. When the public tired of seeing the destitute every day, the police were often told to drive them into less visible locations. As far as I know, nobody has tried to count the number of people living in such semiofficial shelters. But if I am right that communities became less tolerant of such arrangements in the late 1980s, the pressure on the homeless to use shelters presumably increased.

As new shelters became available, two things happened. First, some families that would otherwise have been doubled up in conventional housing moved into shelters. By the late 1980s about 20,000 families with children were living in shelters and welfare hotels.[16] Homeless families with children hardly ever spend the night on the streets, so when they grow more numerous the shelter count rises faster than the street count. New and better shelters also attracted some single adults who once slept in public places.

Irwin Garfinkel and Irving Piliavin have surveyed all the local studies that tried to count the homeless outside shelters between 1983 and 1992.[17] (There were no such surveys before 1983.) These studies were carried out in different cities using different methods, but they tell such a consistent story that they cannot be ignored. Only a minority of the homeless used shelters in 1983. Shelter use remained low between 1983 and 1985. After 1985 the rate of shelter use climbed fairly steadily. By 1990 shelter counts always exceeded street counts. Although I believe these studies all miss a fair number of people outside shelters, a consistent bias of that kind should not invalidate Garfinkel and Piliavin's conclusions about trends over time. My estimates of the street-to-shelter ratio therefore start with Burt's 1987 survey. I then adjust this estimate upward or downward, depending on the year.

Table 2 shows the results of my calculations. My best guess—and it is only an educated guess—is that the homeless population grew from a bit over 100,000 in 1980 to around 200,000 in 1984 and 400,000 in 1987–88. All these figures are far lower than most advocacy groups have claimed, but the trend is familiar, namely up.

Table 2. Number of Individuals Who Were Homeless during an Average Week,
1980–1990

Sleeping place and family type	March 1980	Jan. 1984	1987–88	March 1990
SHELTERS[a]				
Members of families				
with children	<500	13,000[b]	65,000	52,000
Single adults	35,000	57,000[b]	115,000	118,000
Total	35,000	70,000	180,000	170,000
PUBLIC PLACES[c]				
Members of families				
with children	<500	<500	1,000	1,000
Single adults	86,000	140,000	209,000	144,000
CONVENTIONAL HOUSING	4,000	6,000	12,000	9,000
GRAND TOTAL	125,000	216,000	402,000	324,000

Source: See Appendix 1. Estimates exclude children under the age of eighteen not accompanied
by an adult and are rounded to the nearest thousand.

a. Includes hotel rooms paid for with vouchers for the homeless starting in 1987.

b. Assumes that couples without children constituted 10 percent of all families in shelters in
1984, just as they did in 1988.

c. Includes outdoor locations, publicly accessible buildings, abandoned buildings, subways,
automobiles, and other places not intended for sleeping.

Table 2 also suggests that the homeless population declined somewhat between 1987–88 and 1990. This is not surprising. One would
expect homelessness to have declined by the end of the 1980s, since
unemployment was at its lowest level in twenty years. Nonetheless, I
do not have much confidence that this decline really occurred. It is true
that after excluding those in cheap hotels and runaway shelters the
Census Bureau's 1990 shelter count is slightly lower than HUD's 1987–
88 estimate, but that could be due to random sampling error in the
1987–88 survey.[18] It is also true that Garfinkel and Piliavin's data suggest
that the street-to-shelter ratio fell between 1988 and 1990, but their
trend estimates may not hold for these particular years.

The 1980s versus the 1950s

To get a clearer picture of the forces that determine both shelter use
and the overall rate of homelessness, it is instructive to compare two
surveys of Chicago conducted almost thirty years apart. The first was

carried out by Donald Bogue, a University of Chicago demographer who surveyed the city's five skid-row areas in the winter of 1958.[19] He estimated that 975 people slept in the city's missions on a typical winter night and that another 110 people spent the night in public places.[20] In addition, he found 320 skid-row residents in Chicago's jails and hospitals. Even if we assume that half these individuals came from a mission or from the streets, Table 3 shows that by today's standards Chicago had no more than 1300 homeless adults in 1958.

Peter Rossi counted Chicago's homeless again in the fall of 1985. Chicago's largest skid-row area had been torn down by 1985, police practices had changed, and the homeless were now more spread out across the city. To find them, Rossi had his interviewers search a random sample of city blocks during the small hours of the morning, looking in every space they could reach without encountering a locked door or a security guard. This was potentially dangerous work, so interviewers worked in pairs and were accompanied by off-duty policemen. The interviewers asked everyone they found, awake or asleep, whether they had a home elsewhere. (Nine out of ten said they did.) Like Burt, Rossi paid his respondents, so almost everyone answered his questions. Table 3 shows what he found.

Rossi calculated that on a typical September night 1383 adults were sleeping either on the streets or in publicly accessible buildings such as bus stations, airports, all-night movie theaters, and restaurants. He found another 1186 homeless adults in shelters and hospitals. That brought the total number of homeless adults to 2569, which was about twice the number Bogue had counted in similar places.

Rossi also reports that Chicago had 273 homeless children in 1985–86. I do not know what happened to homeless families with children in Chicago during the 1950s. I have been told both that they were moved into public housing and that the children were often taken from their parents and put into foster care. Either way, few were homeless by today's standards. Yet that conclusion dramatizes the danger of taking labels too literally, since my guess is that children in foster care are even more likely to feel homeless than children in family shelters. That does not mean we should start counting every child in foster care as homeless, but we should remember that what we call homelessness is not always the worst thing that can happen to a child (or, indeed, to an adult).

Table 3. Number of Homeless Persons in Chicago, 1958 and 1985–86

Age and location	Bogue: Winter 1958	Rossi: Fall 1985	Rossi: Winter 1986
HOMELESS ADULTS			
General-purpose shelters	975	961	1492
Shelters for battered women and the disabled	0	145[a]	145[a]
Public places	110	1383	528
Hospitals	75[b]	80[c]	80[c]
Jails	85[c]	?	?
Total	1305	2569	2245
HOMELESS CHILDREN	0	273[c]	273[c]
TOTAL HOMELESS	1305	2842	2518
ADULTS IN CUBICLE HOTELS	8000	400[d]	400[d]
GRAND TOTAL	9305	3242	2918

Source: Rossi, pp. 63, 65, 91; Bogue, p 84.

a. Assumes all available beds were occupied.

b. Bogue found 150 city hospital patients and 170 jail inmates with skid-row addresses. I arbitrarily assumed that half of them were living in missions or public places when hospitalized or arrested.

c. Average for fall and winter.

d. Estimated capacity of the two remaining cubicle hotels in 1992.

At the time Rossi did his first survey, advocacy groups claimed Chicago had between 15,000 and 25,000 homeless residents. These groups did their best to discredit Rossi's estimates, which were far lower. But during the winter of 1986 Rossi did a second survey, which yielded even lower numbers than his fall survey (see Table 3). Rossi believes the apparent decline in homelessness between the fall and winter was due to chance, but it could also have been real. When the weather turns bad, some of the Chicago homeless may move to warmer places. At the same time, those who have been moving back and forth between the streets and conventional housing may make more effort to get along with their family or friends in order to stay off the streets. People with unwanted guests are, in turn, probably more reluctant to evict them during a Chicago winter than during the summer.

Although Rossi found far fewer homeless people than advocacy groups expected, he still found far more than Bogue had found a generation earlier. As Table 3 shows, the big change was not that more people slept in shelters but that more people slept in public places.

Another big change was that in 1958 something like 8000 people slept in what were politely known as cubicle hotels. These hotels housed their patrons in windowless 5-by-7-foot rooms, furnished with a bed, a chair, and a bare lightbulb. Rooms were separated by wooden walls and ventilated through wire mesh near the ceiling and floor. Because of the wire mesh, such places were popularly known as cage hotels. They were always noisy, usually verminous, and frequently smelled of urine, vomit, or both.

Nonetheless, almost all skid-row residents preferred these hotels to the free missions run by evangelists. The missions were cleaner, but a cubicle of one's own, however small and noisy, provided more privacy and security than the open dormitory rooms in a mission. The cubicle hotels also treated their patrons more like paying guests and less like charity cases, allowing them to come and go as they pleased and making no effort to improve their character. A cubicle cost roughly $2 to $4 a night in today's money.

Chicago's cubicle hotels housed eight times as many people as its shelters did in 1958. By 1986 Chicago's shelters housed something like three times as many people as its two remaining cubicle hotels did. Thus while the great majority of Chicago's poorest citizens had a private place of their own in 1958, that was no longer true in 1986. Almost all accounts suggest that this pattern recurred in many other cities. The puzzle we need to solve, therefore, is not just why more people lived in public places during the 1980s than during the 1950s, but why fewer people lived in the cage hotels that had traditionally served men with hardly any money.

3. Emptying the Back Wards

As soon as Americans noticed more panhandlers and bag ladies on the streets, they began trying to explain the change. Since the most noticeable of these people behaved in quite bizarre ways, and since everyone knew that state mental hospitals had been sending their chronic patients "back to the community," many sidewalk sociologists initially assumed that the new homeless were mostly former hospital inmates.

Taken literally, that theory turned out to be wrong. Table 4 shows that less than a quarter of the homeless have spent time in a mental hospital. But this is not the right way to assess the impact of deinstitutionalization. Although deinstitutionalization mostly meant that patients were released from mental hospitals after a few weeks instead of remaining there for months, years, or even a lifetime, it also meant that some people who would once have been sent to a mental hospital were now sent to the psychiatric service of a general hospital or were treated as out-patients. It follows that considerably more than a quarter of today's homeless might have spent time in a mental hospital if we still ran the system the way we ran it in the 1950s.

Who Is Mentally Ill?

Freud thought that health meant the ability to work and to love. By that standard the homeless are often in bad shape. A third of the Chicago homeless told Rossi they could not work because of "mental illness" or "nervous problems." Another 10 percent said they could not work

Table 4. Percent of Homeless Adults with Selected Characteristics

Characteristic	Large cities, 1987	All local surveys, 1981–88
Demographic		
Male	84%	74%
Black	45	44
Hispanic	10	12
Over 65	3	na
Mental health		
Spent time in mental hospital	22	24
Attempted suicide	24	na
Diagnosed as currently mentally ill	na	33
Substance abuse		
Currently addicted to alcohol	na	27
Spent time in residential treatment program	na	29
Social ties		
Never married	53	na
Not currently with a spouse	97[a]	na
No friends	na	36
No contact with relatives	na	31
Spent time in jail or prison	41	41
Current health "fair" or "poor" (self-report)	44	38

Source: Column 1 is the weighted mean of estimates for service users and nonusers in cities of 100,000 or more, taken from Martha Burt and Barbara Cohen, *America's Homeless: Numbers, Characteristics, and the Programs That Service Them* (Washington: Urban Institute Press, 1989), pp. 69–71. Column 2 is the unweighted mean of 14 to 40 local surveys, depending on the measure, and comes from Anne Shlay and Peter Rossi, "Social Science Research and Contemporary Studies of Homelessness," *Annual Review of Sociology*, 18 (1992), 129–160. Many of Shlay and Rossi's samples are restricted to shelter residents, who are more likely to be women and tend to be in better mental and physical health than those not in shelters.

a. Adults using shelters or soup kitchens.

because of alcoholism.[1] Only 6 percent of Burt's homeless respondents had steady jobs.[2] While more could have found steady work in a tighter labor market, the homeless are clearly the last hired and the first fired.

The homeless have almost as much trouble maintaining relationships with loved ones as with employers. More than half the Chicago homeless told Rossi that they had no good friends, and 36 percent reported no friends at all. A third also said they had no contact with their relatives, even though they almost all had kin in the Chicago area.[3]

Table 4 shows that the homeless in other cities were also quite isolated. Less than half had ever married, and only 3 percent were still with their spouse at the time they were interviewed.

Some advocates argue that these problems are a byproduct of homelessness itself. That is surely true in some cases. When natural disaster or war drives randomly selected people from their homes, many become acutely depressed, and some grow suicidal or have mental breakdowns. When economic misfortune drives people from their homes, they are even more likely to have such reactions, because they are more likely to blame themselves for their fate.

This argument should not be overdone, however. Rossi asked the Chicago homeless whether they had had any of the following experiences within the past year:

- Hearing noises or voices that others cannot hear.
- Having visions or seeing things that others cannot see.
- Feeling you have special powers that other people do not have.
- Feeling your mind has been taken over by forces you cannot control.

About a third of those whom Rossi interviewed reported having at least one of these delusions at a time when they were neither drunk nor taking drugs.[4] Even when victims of famine and war spend years in refugee camps far worse than any Chicago shelter, no one has ever reported that a third of them saw visions or heard voices. The fact that a third of the Chicago homeless suffer from such delusions must mean, therefore, that a lot of them had such problems before they became homeless.[5]

How many of these people would have been hospitalized in earlier times? Even in the mid-1950s, when the United States hospitalized a larger fraction of its population for mental illness than at any other period in its history, some avoided this fate. A schizophrenic woman who lived quietly with her parents was not likely to be hospitalized if her parents wanted her at home. Nor was a skid-row resident who muttered to invisible strangers likely to be hospitalized if he paid his rent and kept to himself.[6]

When the mentally ill became homeless, however, their chances of landing in a state hospital rose sharply. Free missions seldom took men and women who appeared to be crazy. Since sleeping in public places was illegal, the homeless mentally ill had a lot of contact with the police. If they had no fixed address and acted crazy, they were usually taken to a state hospital for evaluation. Most admitting psychiatrists assumed that anyone who showed signs of mental illness and could not keep a roof over his or her head needed professional care. The homeless mentally ill were therefore quite likely to be locked up even if they were only mildly disturbed from a clinical viewpoint.

Clinicians who examine the homeless today usually conclude that about a third have "severe" mental disorders. Since the homeless were often hospitalized in the 1950s even when their symptoms did not reach this threshold, well over a third of today's homeless might have been locked up at that time. Recreating the mental-health system of the 1950s would therefore cut today's homeless population dramatically. No one believes that such a change would benefit most of the mentally ill, but it might benefit some of those who are now homeless.

The Many Faces of Deinstitutionalization

Before blaming homelessness on deinstitutionalization, however, we must explain one awkward fact: hospitalization rates for mental illness began to fall in the late 1950s, not in the late 1970s or early 1980s. Since deinstitutionalization caused very little homelessness from 1955 to 1975, how could it have suddenly begun to cause a lot of homelessness after that? The answer is that deinstitutionalization was not a single policy but a series of different policies, all of which sought to reduce the number of patients in state mental hospitals but each of which did so by moving these patients to a different place. The policies introduced before 1975 worked quite well. Those introduced after 1975 worked very badly.

Figure 1 shows the progress of deinstitutionalization from 1950 to 1990. The broken line shows how many people would have been in state mental hospitals on an average night if adults' chances of being admitted and discharged had remained constant. The solid line shows the actual numbers. The gap between the two lines provides a rough measure of how many people who would have slept in a state hospital under the

1950 rules slept elsewhere in later years.[7] I refer to these people as having been deinstitutionalized. Readers should remember, however, that some of them never set foot in a mental hospital. They are deinstitutionalized only in the sense that people like them would have been in state hospitals in 1950.[8] Readers should also remember that some of the people I describe as deinstitutionalized merely moved to another institution, such as the psychiatric service of a general hospital, a nursing homes, or a halfway house. Although these individuals have not been deinstitutionalized in the strict sense, no better term seems to exist.

The initial impetus for deinstitutionalization arose in the late 1940s and early 1950s, when the intellectual leaders of the psychiatric profession became convinced that hospitalizing patients who were undergoing an acute episode of mental illness often did more harm than good. That observation had two implications. First, anyone who could be cared for as an out-patient should be. Second, when patients with episodic mental illnesses had to be hospitalized, they should be discharged as soon as possible. The history of deinstitutionalization is the story of America's

Figure 1. Mental Patients in State Hospitals, 1959–1990

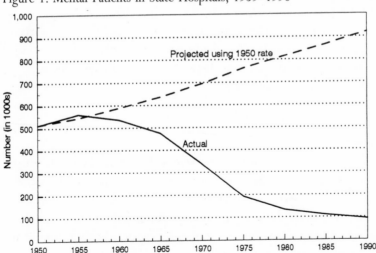

Source: Projections are based on the rate of growth in the civilian, noninstitutional population aged 14 and over. Actual counts for 1950–1985 are taken from David Mechanic and David Rochefort, "Deinstitutionalization: An Appraisal of Reform," *Annual Review of Sociology,* 16 (1990), 307. The 1990 estimate was provided by NIMH.

collective search for other places to send these disturbed and disturbing people.

In a few places (notably Great Britain and Massachusetts), the first round of deinstitutionalization began in the late 1940s and early 1950s, as psychiatrists changed their recommendations for treatment. In most states, however, the process did not gather momentum until the mid-1950s, when the advent of new drugs made out-patient treatment much easier. Thorazine, which became widely available in 1955, did not cure anyone and ultimately produced grisly side effects in some patients, but it did reduce hallucinations and paranoia, making it somewhat easier for families to care for their schizophrenic relatives. Thorazine and its cousins also allowed more schizophrenics to live on their own. Antidepressants also became available during this period and had dramatic effects on some victims of acute depression. Lithium, which was in widespread use by the mid-1960s, had a similar impact on many manic-depressive patients. After lithium, progress in psychopharmacology slowed.

Figure 1 suggests that if admission and discharge rates had not changed, the number of state hospital inmates would have risen from 513,000 in 1950 to 635,000 in 1965. In fact, the number fell to 475,000. One could argue, therefore, that the revolution in psychopharmacology cut the number of people in state hospitals by 25 percent. But that overstates the effect of drugs per se. Part of the decline simply reflected psychiatrists' growing skepticism about the benefits of hospitalization.

Alternative Institutions

The second round of deinstitutionalization began in 1965, when Congress established Medicaid to cover the bills of many poor patients. Congress did not want the federal government to assume responsibility for patients whose bills were already being paid by the states, so Medicaid did not cover anyone in a state mental hospital; but it did cover short-term psychiatric care in general hospitals. As a result, the proportion of poor patients getting short-term care from state hospitals began to fall, while the proportion getting care from the psychiatric service of a general hospital rose.

Medicaid also covered patients in nursing homes. In an effort to prevent mass transfers from state mental hospitals to nursing homes, Medicaid rules excluded nursing homes that provided psychiatric care. But before 1965 indigent patients had often been sent to state mental hospitals even when their problems were primarily physical, simply because these hospitals were free. Once Medicaid became available, states began transferring as many of these patients as possible to nursing homes, in order to shift part of the bill to Washington. Many of these homes provided even worse medical care than the state hospitals, but both patients and their families preferred them nonetheless, because the other residents were saner. In the end, the shift from state hospitals to nursing homes was probably driven as much by consumer choice as by state policy.[9]

Like the effects of new drugs, the effects of Medicaid were accentuated by changing professional attitudes. By the mid-1960s the young psychiatric residents who made day-to-day decisions about admitting and releasing patients were increasingly likely to believe not only that patients suffering from short-term problems would recover faster if they could be kept out of a hospital, but that even "chronics" would be better off living with their families or in residential hotels. Americans were also growing more tolerant of bizarre behavior, so state hospitals were under less political and social pressure to lock up everyone who acted crazy. Gradual increases in public-assistance benefits also made it easier for the mentally ill to survive outside hospitals.

Congress set off a third round of deinstitutionalization in 1972, when it established Supplemental Security Income (ssi). ssi provided a federally financed monthly check for everyone whom the Social Security Administration judged incapable of holding a job because of a physical or mental disability. Recipients also got food stamps and a Medicaid card, and their cash benefits rose automatically with inflation. In 1992 the combined value of federal ssi payments and food stamps was about $500 a month.

Inmates of state mental hospitals became eligible for ssi as soon as they were discharged. That gave states a new financial incentive to move the mentally ill out of hospitals. ssi also made it easier for poor families to care for their disturbed relatives, and it allowed some mildly disturbed patients to live on their own. If the mentally ill could not care for themselves and had no relatives who were willing and able to do so, SSI made it easier to place them in private "board and care" facilities (which are just nursing homes without nurses). When patients entered such a facility, they usually signed over their SSI check to the management and lived pretty much as they would have lived on the chronic ward of a state hospital: eating, sleeping, taking their medication, watching television, playing cards, and staring into space. But now Washington paid most of the bills.

SSI was conceived primarily as a program for people who were too old or too physically disabled to work and whose past earnings had been so low that they got little or nothing from Social Security. Congress never expected SSI to cover the full cost of caring for people with serious mental disorders. At $500 a month, SSI is enough to keep the frugal elderly off the streets. (Only about 10,000 people over the age of sixty-five appear to have been homeless in 1987–88.[10]) But $500 a month will not pay for much beyond room and board, so a facility that relies exclusively on SSI to pay residents' bills cannot afford to admit anyone who requires much staff attention. If such a place admits the mentally ill, it must restrict itself to patients who can care for themselves and who cause no trouble. In order to do more, it needs extra money from the state for extra staff.

Figure 1 shows that the number of adults in state mental hospitals fell 60 percent between 1965 and 1975. Many elderly mental patients moved to nursing homes. Many younger mental patients returned to their families. Others ended up living alone or in board-and-care facilities.[11] If there was a significant increase in homelessness during this era, no one commented on it.

By 1975 most state hospitals had discharged almost everyone they thought they could house elsewhere. Their 200,000-odd remaining inmates were of two kinds: long-term residents who were so disturbed nobody else would take them, and short-term patients who were admitted, medicated, observed for a couple of weeks, and discharged. Some of these short-term patients were readmitted fairly regularly, often because they stopped taking their medication, but they spent the bulk of their time outside hospitals.

While patients often cycled in and out of mental hospitals in the early 1970s, relatively few hospitals discharged patients who had nowhere to go. That was because the police in most states still brought those who ended up on the streets back to the hospital that had discharged them. The psychiatric staff saw no point in discharging patients who would be back in a matter of days. Readmission required a lot of paperwork, so it was easier just to keep these patients in the hospital.

The End of Involuntary Commitment

Although the number of patients in state mental hospitals fell from 468 per 100,000 adults in 1950 to 119 in 1975, advocates of deinstitutionalization were far from satisfied. Rather than simply continuing their campaign to alter physicians' clinical judgments about who should be hospitalized, reformers increasingly turned to the courts, challenging physicians' right to commit anyone at all. These challenges began to influence medical practice in some states during the early 1970s, but their main impact came in the late 1970s, when they precipitated a fourth round of deinstitutionalization.

During the 1960s writers like Erving Goffman, Thomas Szasz, R. D. Laing, and Michel Foucault tried to convince the public that mental hospitals were oppressive places and that psychiatrists were agents of social control. Since many mental hospitals really did deprive patients of rights accorded almost every other human being, and since the therapeutic rationales offered for many hospital rules seemed unpersuasive, many people (including me) found these antiauthoritarian critiques quite persuasive. By the early 1970s most civil-liberties lawyers endorsed Szasz's argument that we should lock up the mentally ill only if they broke the law. The Supreme Court encouraged such thinking throughout the 1970s. In 1975, for example, the Court ruled in *O'Connor v. Donaldson* that mental illness alone was not sufficient justification for involuntary commitment. By the end of the 1970s almost every state had made it impossible to lock up patients for more than a few days unless they posed a clear danger to themselves or others.

This was a sharp break with the past. The Anglo-American conception of individual rights rests partly on the premise that each of us is the best judge of our own interests. This assumption leads directly to the idea that adults should be free to manage their own lives so long as their behavior does not threaten others. But even those with a strong commitment to individual rights usually made exceptions for people who did not seem to know their own interests. Among these people were children, the mentally retarded, and those we called insane, crazy, mad, or mentally ill. Endowing such individuals with the full panoply of legal rights that we gave a "rational" adult was thought dangerous, both to the recipients and to others.

Limiting the rights of the mentally ill on the grounds that they are too confused to know their own interests or to respect the rights of others led to many abuses. But the fact that a principle is often abused does not mean it is wrong. The presumption that parents know their children's interests better than the children do has also been widely abused, but it does not follow that children are better off when they can run their lives as they please. Like the line between childhood and adulthood, the line between sanity and insanity is fuzzy. But it does not follow that mental illness is merely a myth invented to keep deviants in line, any more than childhood is. The boundary separating India from China is also uncertain and contested, but hardly anyone doubts that Calcutta is in India or that Shanghai is in China.

For the civil-liberties lawyers who led the fight against involuntary commitment, all this was irrelevant. They thought individual autonomy so important that they could hardly imagine patients who would be better off when other people told them what to do. They also identified so strongly with the oppressed that they could not take seriously the idea that releasing mentally ill patients from hospitals might make the rest of us worse off.

Many other people supported restrictions on involuntary commitment for more sensible reasons. Some thought mental hospitals were bound to be bad for patients, because forcing the mentally ill to live with one another made them even crazier. Others thought mental hospitals could become therapeutic institutions, but only if staff members stopped relying on coercion to change patients' behavior. These reformers, who included experienced therapists as well as lawyers, hoped that curtailing involuntary commitment would force hospitals to do their job better. Unlike most of the hopes raised by deinstitutionalization, this one was actually realized. Almost everyone agrees that curtailing involuntary commitment improved the quality of life inside mental hospitals, just as almost everyone agrees that it reduced the quality of life outside them.

Once America restricted involuntary commitment, many seriously · disturbed patients began leaving state hospitals even when they had nowhere else to live. When their mental condition deteriorated, as it periodically did, these patients were also free to break off contact with the mental-health system. In many cases they also broke with the friends and relatives who had helped them deal with public agencies. The mentally ill are seldom adept at dealing with such agencies on their own, so once they lost touch with the people who had acted as their advocates, they often lost (or never got) the disability benefits to which they were theoretically entitled. In due course some ended up not only friendless but penniless and homeless.

The Dangerous Mentally Ill

In theory, psychiatrists can still lock up people who pose a danger to themselves or others. In practice, legal and budgetary changes have made this less common than it used to be. A recent study by Daniel Martell and Park Elliott Dietz provides a vivid illustration of how casually the mental health system now deals with mental patients who engage in violence.[12]

Martell and Dietz studied thirty-two individuals arrested between 1975 and 1991 for trying to push a stranger onto the New York City subway tracks. The police referred twenty-six of these people for psychiatric evaluation. Martell and Dietz tried to follow up these cases. The New York state mental-health system had no records for six of the twenty-six offenders referred to it. Of the twenty offenders whose records the state could locate, nineteen had been diagnosed as psychotic. All nineteen had been hospitalized before, and thirteen had previous arrests for violent crimes. Yet even those whose histories included both psychotic delusions and violent crimes had all been released. Half were homeless at the time they pushed their victim onto the tracks.

The reader might think that these were precisely the kinds of people who should be subject to involuntary commitment. They were clearly crazy. They had histories of violence. Their behavior posed a danger to others. So why were they released? The answer seems to be partly legal and partly budgetary.

Legally, it is now impossible to lock people up forever simply because they were both psychotic and violent at some time in the past. If they are no longer psychotic today—if, that is, physicians are willing to say they have recovered—they are entitled to another chance. The fact that people with histories of schizophrenia and violence tend to have relapses, when they once again lash out at others, does not have a comfortable place in American legal thinking. America has always been a land of second chances. Violent psychotics now get a second chance just like everyone else.

Even when a legal case can be made for long-term confinement, fiscal austerity makes it rare except in the most extreme cases. If mental hospitals are trying to close wards, they have a strong incentive to decide that asymptomatic patients have recovered, no matter what the patient's past history suggests about the likelihood of a recurrence. Discharging such patients might not pose a great danger to others if they could be monitored closely after leaving the hospital. But monitoring out-patients is difficult even when they have stable housing, and it is impossible when they have no fixed address. That is presumably one reason why Martell and Dietz found that the risk of being pushed onto the subway tracks was three times as high in the 1980s as in the late 1970s.

Something has gone badly wrong with a system that produces these results. Part of the problem is that we now have too few beds in state mental hospitals. But we also seem to have forgotten a fundamental truth about society, namely that someone has to be responsible for every individual's actions. In most cases, of course, we hold adults responsible for their own actions. But when people are too young, too retarded, or too deranged to be held responsible, society has to designate someone else to assume responsibility. When people's relatives cannot or will not play this role, society needs to create an institution to act *in loco parentis*. This institution needs the same broad discretionary powers that parents have over their children, not the more circumscribed powers that courts have over those whom they can punish for their sins after the fact. For patients with a history of violence, that discretionary power probably has to include preventive detention.

Yet while we need to do something about the fact that mental patients with histories of violence often end up homeless, we should not exaggerate the magnitude of this problem.[13] The homeless mentally ill are probably a bit more prone to violence than the average American, but they are by no means the most dangerous people on the streets. Indeed, while I know no statistics on the matter, I suspect that when the homeless mentally ill are involved in violence they are as likely to be victims as aggressors. Assaults on the homeless in general and the homeless mentally ill in particular are common throughout the United States. In a growing number of cases, supposedly sane people have set the homeless afire. Even Martell and Dietz found that while most of the individuals who pushed someone onto the subway track were mentally ill and many were homeless, there were three incidents in which gangs of youths had pushed a homeless individual onto the tracks.

The Tax Revolt

Soon after the rules restricting involuntary commitment began taking effect, a nationwide tax revolt precipitated a fifth round of deinstitutionalization. Faced with rising costs and slow growth in their tax base, state governors and legislators kept pressing mental hospitals to trim their budgets. Most hospitals responded by closing wards. These hospitals had already transferred all the chronic patients they could house elsewhere. The only way they could close more wards was to cut the time short-term patients spent in the hospital or discharge chronic patients who had nowhere else to go.

Hospitals had started discharging chronic patients with nowhere to go because the courts said these patients had a legal right to leave. But once the taboo was broken, the practice soon spread to patients who had not insisted on leaving. As time went on, even patients who were willing to stay in the hospital got pushed out, on the grounds that a hospital was not a hotel. Today some state hospitals do not even bother to discharge such patients. They simply write a weekend pass and tell the patient not to come back.

States could have kept most of the mentally ill off the streets by finding them rented rooms and paying the rent directly to the landlord. But once civil libertarians endowed the mentally ill with the same legal rights as everyone else, state politicians felt free to endow them with the same legal responsibilities as everyone else, including responsibility for paying their own rent. The mentally ill are seldom good at planning ahead or managing their money, so even those who got monthly disability checks were often unwilling or unable to set aside enough money for rent. Those who did not get a disability check, or whose checks stopped coming because they failed to file a form or show up for a hearing, had even more trouble paying their rent.

States compounded this problem by cutting their cash payments to the mentally ill. Most states had supplemented federal SSI benefits for the disabled during the 1970s. Almost all states let these supplements lag behind inflation during the 1980s.[14] Some states tried to replace cash SSI payments with various kinds of subsidized housing, but as far as I know no state guaranteed the deinstitutionalized mentally ill a place to live.

This transformation of America's mental-health system could not have happened without two decades of bipartisan propaganda suggesting that deinstitutionalization would save huge sums of money without hurting patients. That claim turned out to be greatly exaggerated. Most experts agree that out-patient care yields better results than equally expensive in-patient care.[15] It seems to follow that one should be able to achieve equally good outcomes at somewhat lower cost using out-patient care. But the general rule is that good care costs quite a lot regardless of where patients sleep. Deinstitutionalization saves big money only when it is followed by gross neglect. That was why neglect became so common during the 1980s.

Mental hospitals are certainly expensive. State mental hospitals spent a total of $7.7 billion dollars to care for about 90,000 patients a day in 1990. That means they were spending about $234 per patient per day.[16] Nursing homes, board-and-care facilities, SROs, and municipal shelters all spent far less. But that does not suffice to prove that mental hospitals are wasting money. They do, after all, perform different functions from all these other institutions. First, they diagnose patients with acute problems, prescribe drugs for them, and make recommendations about their care, which means they need far more doctors, nurses, and paper shufflers than nursing homes, board-and-care facilities, SROs, or shelters. Second, state hospitals provide custodial care for some people who are so disruptive or dangerous that other institutions refuse to deal with them. Any institution that plays this role is bound to need a lot of attendants.

A mental hospital's budget goes to meet its patients' need for three things: subsistence, supervision, and treatment. There is no obvious reason why feeding and housing mental patients should cost more in a hospital than in any other institution. The cost of food and shelter does fall when patients live with their families, but that is not an option for those who concern us here. Shelters staffed by volunteers or board-and-care facilities staffed by minimum-wage workers can put meals on the table and keep floors cleaned more cheaply than state hospitals, but these are economies that harm a society in the long run. Furthermore, the main way that states cut mental patients' subsistence costs is to offer less. Forcing schizophrenics to sleep in group shelters or giving them only one meal a day instead of three does save money—but at what cost?

Mental-health planners have also tried to cut the cost of supervising the mentally ill. Because supervision costs are high in mental hospitals, planners often imagine that it would be cheaper to house hospital patients in less-supervised settings. That makes sense if moving patients to new settings improves their behavior. But if patients go on acting the same way, simply moving them to a new setting is unlikely to save money. If those who were disruptive in the hospital remain disruptive, the board-and-care facility will have to hire more supervisory staff and become more like a hospital. The same will be true if patients are sent to shelters, which is why many shelters refuse to admit them.

Nor will transferring patients who can look after themselves necessarily save money. Suppose a hospital spends $1000 a day supervising a ward with fifty chronic patients, half of whom need constant supervision and half of whom need none. That works out to $20 per patient every day, so transferring the patients who need no supervision to a place that spends a quarter as much seems like an obvious economy. But transferring the patients who require no attention will not in fact cut the cost of running the hospital ward, because demands on the staff will not decline. If the hospital ignores this fact and tries to fill the ward entirely with patients who need a lot of attention, it will soon have to double the ward's staff.

Readers who remember Ken Kesey's *One Flew over the Cuckoo's Nest* may wonder whether mental patients really need all this supervision. In the 1960s, when Kesey wrote, many did not. But by the end of the 1970s state hospitals were discharging almost any patient who could get along without supervision. The patients still living in state hospitals in 1980 were either there for very short periods or needed so much supervision that no other institution would take them.

When mental patients who need supervision do not get it, they often become embroiled in serious conflicts with other people. Some of these conflicts lead them to engage in violence against others. Others lead to violence against the mentally ill. Keeping such patients out of trouble is costly no matter where they live. For most patients the cost will be less than $234 a day. But so long as we have to pay someone to provide care, the cost will be substantial. We can reduce these costs if we harden our hearts and let these lost souls fend for themselves. But that is like feeding people once a day or letting them sleep on a steam grate.

Although hospital planners have tried to cut state spending on subsistence and supervision over the past twenty years, they have not tried as hard to cut expenditures for medical treatment. Discharging chronic patients did not appreciably reduce treatment costs, since these patients seldom saw the medical staff. Cutting the length of stay for new patients made equally little difference, since admitting a patient, deciding on a course of treatment, changing the medication when the initial treatment does not work, discharging the patient, and doing all the relevant paperwork consumes about the same amount of professional time regardless of whether the process is compressed into a week or spread out over several months.

Once we look at what mental hospitals actually do, it becomes easier to see why deinstitutionalization saved less money than its advocates promised. Between 1975 and 1990 state mental hospitals cut the number of patients they sheltered on an average night by 54 percent, but they cut their staffs by only 20 percent, and their real expenditure rose 5 percent.[17]

Federal Cutbacks

Although the Republican Party played a central role in creating the political climate in which deinstitutionalization unfolded during the

1980s, it was unable to cut federal support for the mentally ill anything like as much as it wanted. The Reagan Administration did get Congress to fold federal money for Community Mental Health Centers (CMHCs) into block grants to the states, but that did not appreciably reduce the resources available for treating people with severe mental problems. Indeed, it may have created more such resources.

The CMHCs were created during the 1960s to provide out-patient care for the severely disturbed patients who were being moved out of state hospitals. But since few therapists wanted to work with psychotic patients, the CMHCs soon redefined their role as preventing rather than treating severe mental illness. Under the banner of prevention they began working with patients who were depressed, angry, anxious, or in the midst of some family crisis, paying little attention to schizophrenics. After 1981, when Reagan made CMHC funding a state responsibility, some CMHCs decided that their best hope for survival was to treat more psychotics. By caring for people who would otherwise be in a state hospital, they could claim that they were saving the state money. That may also have been true when they worked with less disturbed patients, but the case was harder to make because the payoff was farther in the future.

The Reagan Administration also tried to tighten eligibility standards for federal disability benefits. The percentage of working-age adults getting disability benefits had risen steadily during the 1970s. Even before Reagan was elected, Congress had told the Social Security Administration that it should conduct periodic reviews to see if disabled beneficiaries were still unable to work. Two months after Reagan took office, the SSA accelerated this process and began purging the disability rolls of people it judged capable of working. Many of these reviews were scandalously perfunctory. Some 300,000 people were dropped from the rolls between 1981 and 1983, including perhaps 100,000 with mental problems.[18] Very few found work.[19] Some presumably became homeless.

This assault on the disabled was one of the low points of modern American social policy, but it did not last long. In mid-1983, after hundreds of lawsuits and a great deal of bad publicity, the SSA suspended its effort to purge the rolls. By the time Reagan left office, the fraction of the working-age population collecting disability benefits was as high as it had been in 1980.[20] The fraction of new beneficiaries with mental rather than physical disabilities was also twice as high in the late 1980s as it had been a decade earlier.[21] Thus the percentage of working-age adults getting federal benefits for a mental disability was higher at the end of the 1980s than ever before in American history.

Why should the number of people getting benefits for a mental disability have grown during a period when the administration was trying to cut back? Some conservatives think that civil servants who made eligibility decisions grew more soft-hearted with the passing of time. So far as I have been able to discover, no lawyer who actually dealt with the Social Security Administration during the 1980s believes this. A more convincing explanation, I think, is that many other traditional sources of support for the mentally ill were drying up during the 1980s, making more people eligible for federal benefits.

States cut the proportion of adults living in state mental hospitals from 76 per 100,000 in 1980 to 47 per 100,000 in 1990. Almost all these people became eligible for disability benefits. States were also trying to cut their expenditures on General Assistance (GA), which provides state money to jobless adults who do not qualify for any kind of federal support. One way states cut GA was to help recipients qualify for SSI disability benefits, which came largely from Washington.

Meanwhile, a combination of legal and illegal immigration was creating more competition for casual unskilled jobs. In the past, men with episodic mental problems had often taken such jobs when they were asymptomatic. Even occasional work made them ineligible for disability benefits. As casual jobs became harder to get, the fraction of the mentally ill who had not worked for a year rose, making more of them eligible for benefits. The deinstitutionalized mentally ill also began using crack in significant numbers after 1985. That not only reduced their chances of finding work but often made their symptoms worse, increasing their chance of qualifying for benefits.

What Went Wrong?

Although the federal government spent more to support people with severe mental illnesses in 1990 than in 1980, the increase was clearly inadequate to offset the effect of changes in the way states ran their hospitals. The best available data suggest that in 1987 at least 1.7 million working-age Americans had mental problems so severe they could not hold a job.[22] Roughly 100,000 of these people were homeless. No other affluent country has abandoned its mentally ill to this extent.

If the courts had not limited involuntary commitment and if state hospitals had not started discharging patients with nowhere to go, the proportion of the adult population living in state hospitals would probably be about the same today as in 1975. Were that the case, state hospitals would have sheltered 234,000 mental patients on an average night in 1990 rather than 92,000. It follows that 142,000 people who would have been sleeping in a state hospital under the 1975 rules were sleeping somewhere else by 1990. On any given night, some of these people were in the psychiatric wards of general hospitals, and a few were in private psychiatric hospitals, but many were in shelters or on the streets.

Almost everyone agrees that what happened to the mentally ill after 1975 was a disaster. Both liberals and conservatives blame this disaster on their opponents, and both are half right. It was the insidious combination of liberal policies aimed at increasing personal liberty with conservative policies aimed at reducing government spending that led to catastrophe. It is important to remember, however, that while liberals succeeded in curtailing involuntary commitment and deinstitutionalizing most of the mentally ill, their conservative opponents failed to cut government spending on mental patients. All the conservatives did was slow the rate of budgetary growth.

The bulk of state mental-health budgets has always gone to hospitals, and that did not change during the 1980s. Measured in 1990 dollars, state hospitals spent $7.7 billion in 1990, up from $6.5 billion in 1979.[23] Expenditures on residential services for out-patients also rose. Measured in constant dollars, the average state spent about $50 a month for each out-patient in 1987 compared to $30 in 1981.[24] Such sums were obviously inadequate, but the trend was up. The main area where states cut back was in their ssi supplements. Measured in 1992 dollars, the median state supplement fell from $74 a month in 1980 to $32 a month in 1992.[25]

Statistics of this kind suggest that the problems of the mentally ill were at least partly traceable to political and institutional inertia. States could have cut their hospital spending substantially by merging or closing hospitals. But local legislators fought hard to prevent this, so states kept most mental hospitals open and let them serve fewer patients. Hospitals could also have served the mentally ill better if they had continued to offer custodial care for patients with nowhere else to live. But those who ran state hospitals were professionally committed to the idea that they should provide better treatment rather than running a better hotel. This stance was reenforced by self-interest. Spending more on treatment and less on subsistence allowed those who cared for the mentally ill to improve their standard of living at a time when the mentally ill themselves were experiencing more material hardship.[26]

Needless to say, the mental-health establishment does not see the last twenty years in these terms. From its perspective, the continuing shift from in-patient to out-patient care made medical sense. The problem was that callous state legislators refused to appropriate enough money for out-patient programs. In a sense, this analysis is correct. But it says nothing about where the extra money for out-patient care should have come from. Assuming that out-patient care is no more expensive than in-patient care, the answer seems clear: the money should have come from state hospital budgets.

While deinstitutionalizing the mentally ill should not save much money overall, it should allow states to shift resources from in-patient to out-patient services. No realist expects hospitals themselves to propose such changes, but state governors and legislators could have done so. The number of mental patients sleeping in state hospitals fell by 100,000 between 1975 and 1990. Had politicians been committed to keeping the mentally ill off the streets, they could have used the money that hospitals once spent on these patients to provide SRO rooms and out-patient services. Some states did try this. In most states, however, political leaders mouthed clichés and looked the other way.

4. The Crack Epidemic

While deinstitutionalization of the mentally ill was the most widely cited explanation for homelessness in the early 1980s, drugs got more attention later in the decade. Until the mid-1980s, the very poor had relied largely on alcohol to forget their troubles. This was not because they all found alcohol more satisfying than other mind-altering chemicals; it was just cheaper. Indeed, hard drugs were so expensive that many surveys of the homeless in the early 1980s did not even bother to ask about the subject. When interviewers did ask, the homeless were far more likely to report alcohol than drug problems.

Alcoholism has been a significant cause of homelessness for generations, but I found no good evidence that it became more common during the 1980s, either in the nation as a whole or among the very poor. Surveys of the homeless conducted in the early 1980s typically concluded that about a third of them had serious alcohol problems.[1] Surveys of skid-row residents earlier in the century usually came up with similar figures. Thus if our task is to explain why the very poor have moved from skid-row hotels to shelters and the streets over the past generation, alcohol is not a promising explanation.

The arrival of crack in the mid-1980s changed this picture substantially. Crack produced a shorter high than earlier forms of cocaine, but it was also much cheaper. When it arrived on the streets in the mid-1980s, a single hit typically cost $10. Today the price is often $5 and sometimes as low as $3. Like the half-pint whiskey bottle, crack made the pleasures of cocaine available to people who had very little cash and were likely to spend it on the first high they could afford. Within a few years, crack was available almost everywhere the homeless congregated.

Antidrug propagandists often try to convince the public that everyone who uses crack becomes an addict, but that is not true. Ethnographic studies suggest that crack users are in fact a lot like alcohol users: some use crack constantly (at least until their money runs out), some use it only occasionally, and some fall in between. Nor is crack necessarily worse for people than alcohol—the jury is still out on that question. But it is clear that some people who were not alcoholics found crack very seductive. That means a society in which people can get both alcohol and crack will have more chemical dependency than a society in which only alcohol is available.

How Many of the Homeless Use Crack?

Surveys that ask people how much alcohol they use always end up with far lower estimates of total consumption than surveys that ask manufacturers how much alcohol they have sold. Because the production and distribution of cocaine is illegal, manufacturers do not provide the Treasury Department with data on their total output. Nonetheless, it seems safe to assume that those who rely on users to provide information about their level of drug consumption will underestimate the extent of the problem.

Unlike surveys, urine samples provide relatively reliable estimates of cocaine use. In 1991 the Cuomo Commission asked a large sample of New York City shelter users for anonymous urine samples. Participation was voluntary. Among single adults in general-purpose shelters who agreed to participate, 66 percent tested positive for cocaine.[2] In family shelters, the figure was 16 percent. According to the commission, earlier surveys that had asked shelter residents direct questions about drug use yielded far lower estimates of cocaine consumption.

Cocaine remains in a user's urine for only two to three days, so the Cuomo Commission's tests missed some occasional users. But while more than two thirds of the single adults in New York shelters probably used crack occasionally, fewer than two thirds were likely to have been daily users.

Since many people assume that New York is the crack capital of the world, and since no other city has collected urine samples from its shelter users, it is tempting to dismiss the Cuomo Commission's findings as atypical. But New York is not as atypical as most people imagine. Among men arrested during 1990 in Manhattan—the only New York borough for which I could find data—65 percent tested positive for cocaine. America has seven other cities with more than a million inhabitants: Los Angeles, Chicago, Houston, Philadelphia, San Diego, Detroit, and Dallas. Among men arrested in these seven cities, 49 percent tested positive for cocaine in 1990.[3] Figures for arrestees in smaller cities are usually lower, but not a lot lower.

New York City's statistics suggest that cocaine use is about as common among single homeless adults in general-purpose shelters as among arrestees. If that rule holds for other cities of more than a million, about half the single men and women who went to shelters in these cities during 1991 had used cocaine within the past couple of days. Nationwide, a reasonable guess might then be that a third of all home-less single adults use crack fairly regularly. If so, crack is now as big a problem among the homeless as alcohol.

New York's general-purpose shelters are notoriously bad places, so the foregoing calculations may somewhat overstate the level of cocaine consumption. But even if only a quarter of the homeless are using crack regularly, it still seems likely that the overall rate of substance abuse among the homeless is higher today than it was in the early 1980s. That may help explain the otherwise puzzling increase in homelessness be-tween 1984 and 1988, when unemployment was falling.

Does Crack Cause Homelessness?

Advocates for the homeless usually argue that drug use, like mental illness, is a product of homelessness. Big-city shelters are full of crack, and so are many of the public places where the homeless gather. In some of these places, sharing drugs has apparently become the nexus of social life, in much the way that sharing a bottle was a decade ago. This could mean that a lot of people begin using crack because they are homeless rather than the other way around.

Just as with mental illness, this line of argument captures an important truth. But just as with mental illness, it also ignores another important truth: heavy drug use can cause homelessness. Heavy use makes marginally employable adults even less employable, eats up money that would otherwise be available to pay rent, and makes their friends and relatives less willing to shelter them. We have no reliable data on how many of the homeless were already heavy users before they became homeless, but the proportion must be higher than in the general population.

Furthermore, while we have no hard evidence about crack's role in pushing people onto the streets, it clearly helps keep them there. Burt found that half the single adults who used shelters or soup kitchens in large cities reported that their cash income for the month prior to being interviewed was less than $70. That works out to about $2.30 a day. Only one in six reported taking in more than $10 a day.[4] Thus if homeless crack users were paying in cash, drugs must have consumed most of their income.

A bed in a New York or Chicago cubicle hotel currently costs about $8 a night. Most people who have enough money to buy substantial amounts of crack could therefore afford to rent a cubicle instead. A large fraction of the single adults in the New York shelters who test positive for cocaine presumably think that a crack high, however brief, is worth more than a scuzzy cubicle.

Some of the homeless may, of course, be getting their crack free because they work for a distributor in some menial capacity. I have no idea how common this is. We badly need more reliable information on where the homeless get their money and how they spend it. But the only way to collect better information is to spend endless hours with the homeless, observing what they do instead of just asking them about such matters on surveys. Living with the homeless is both disagreeable and dangerous, so only the adventurous want to do it. And adventurers seldom want to keep track of other people's money.

Whatever their current budgets look like, we have to assume that a significant proportion of today's homeless will spend any additional cash they receive on drugs or alcohol. This is likely to be true regardless of whether the extra money comes from a government check or from individual handouts. It is hard to be sure how large this group is. It might be as small as a third of the homeless or as large as two thirds.

But even if two thirds of the homeless were using all their extra cash to buy more drugs or alcohol, that would leave a third who were not. One cannot, then, build a case against either public or private charity on statistics of this kind. Only a fool imagines that every dollar spent on doing good has the intended effect. If even a third of the money we give the homeless ends up improving the quality of their lives, it would yield more happiness than most of what we spend on ourselves.

Nonetheless, some conservatives push the argument a step further, claiming that by giving the homeless free shelter we are, in effect, helping them buy more alcohol or drugs. That argument surely contains a grain of truth, but probably not much more than that. Even when shelters are free, fewer than half of all homeless single adults use them on an average night. This makes it hard to believe that eliminating shelters would persuade many homeless drug or alcohol users to spend their limited funds on renting a room. The main effect would probably be to push the proportion who sleep in public places back to what it was in the early 1980s.

We could, of course, revive the traditional practice of jailing people who sleep in public places. But judges who cannot find enough cells for people who steal automobiles and television sets are unlikely to hand out long sentences to those who merely sleep in doorways. If mayors tell the police to arrest such people, judges will have to release them the next day, just as they did thirty years ago. The prospect of a night in jail did deter some alcoholics from spending all their money on drink during the 1950s and 1960s, and it might keep a few drug users from spending all their money on crack in the 1990s. But I see no reason to think that this deterrent effect would be large.

Indeed, jailing people who sleep in public places could conceivably encourage substance abuse. That possibility arises because in some respects jails provide better accommodations than shelters. A survey conducted in New York City during the early 1980s found that those who had spent time in both shelters and jails rated the jails superior to the shelters on cleanliness, safety, privacy, and food quality. Shelters ranked ahead of jails only on personal freedom.[5] Although shelters are probably cleaner and almost certainly provide better food today than in the early 1980s, they offer no more privacy and are probably more dangerous.

Because punishment does so little to deter chemical addiction, liberal reformers usually prefer detox centers and twelve-step programs. The Cuomo Commission strongly endorsed more services of this kind, but neither the Commission's report nor any of the other books I have examined provides convincing evidence about how well these services work. The Commission simply assumed that services would work. Such optimism represents a triumph of hope over experience. Without hope, the world would be a worse place than it is. Still, experience does suggest that while some services work some of the time, many are ineffective. When advocates fail to mention this risk, taxpayers should check their bank balance.

Drugs, Madness, Luck, and Blame

Despite all the evidence that mental illness and substance abuse play a big role in homelessness, some knowledgable people still insist that the homeless are mostly people "just like you and me" who happen to be down on their luck.[6] The homeless are indeed just like you and me in most respects. But so are saints and serial killers. Members of the same species inevitably have a lot in common. We all need food to survive, put on our socks one at a time, remember our childhood with mixed feelings, and worry about dying. But important as such similarities are, our differences are also important. To ignore them when we talk about the homeless is to substitute sentimentality for compassion.[7]

The theory that the homeless have just hit a patch of bad luck is at best a partial truth. Both success and failure are the cumulative product of many influences, of which luck is only one. If you study people who have climbed to the pinnacles of power and influence in American society, you usually find that they have had "all the advantages." Most started life with competent parents, had more than their share of brains, energy, or charm, and then had unusual good luck. Without any one of these advantages they might still have done well, but not as well as they did.

The same rule applies at the bottom of the economic ladder. Those who end up on the street have typically had all the disadvantages. Most started life in families with a multitude of problems; indeed, many came from families so troubled that they were placed in foster care. Many had serious health and learning problems. A large number grew up in dreadful neighborhoods and attended mediocre schools. After that, most had more than their share of bad luck in the labor market, the marriage market, or both. It is the cumulative effect of all these disadvantages, not bad luck alone, that has left them on the streets.

When we try to understand this issue, it helps to remember that if bad luck were the main cause of homelessness, good luck would suffice to end it. Luck is by definition always changing. Thus if bad luck were the main cause of homelessness, most people would be homeless occasionally, but few would be homeless for long. In reality, most people are never homeless, a sizable number are homeless briefly, and a few are homeless for long periods. The long-term homeless are mostly people for whom almost everything imaginable has gone wrong for many years. Many are heavy drug or alcohol users. Many have severe mental disabilities. Even those who do not have such easily labeled problems have the kind of bad luck that recurs over and over, causing them to lose one job after another and one friend after another. In such cases it makes more sense to speak of bad karma than of bad luck.

Sympathetic writers and advocates often dwell on bad luck because they want to convince the public that the homeless are victims of circumstances beyond their control and deserve our help. This strikes me as a myopic strategy. It inspires incredulity among the worldly, and it leads the credulous to underestimate how much help the long-term homeless really need. If bad luck were the main cause of long-term homelessness, we could solve the problem by giving everyone on the street a shower, clean clothes, a job at McDonald's, and a roommate. Sometimes that is all the homeless need, and surely we should offer it. But many need a great deal more.

Debates about the relative importance of luck and character are often just covert arguments about the assignment of blame. Americans have always thought their country perfectible, so when something goes wrong we look for scapegoats. In the case of homelessness, conservatives want to blame the homeless, while liberals want to blame conservatives. Both explanations are correct. If no one drank, took drugs, lost contact with reality, or messed up at work, homelessness would be rare.

If America had a safety net comparable to Sweden's or Germany's, homelessness would also be rare. It is the combination of personal vulnerability and political indifference that has left people in the streets.

In trying to explain this situation, we need to replace our instinctive either-or approach to blame with a both-and approach. Consider drugs. Homelessness spread during the 1980s partly because criminal entrepreneurs made cocaine available in smaller doses at lower cost. They clearly deserve lots of blame. Those who succumbed to this new form of temptation must also take responsibility for what crack did to them. But that does not mean either our culture or our political institutions can escape blame. America has had high levels of drug and alcohol abuse for generations. No one knows exactly why this is, but it is an integral part of our culture. Most societies prepare children for competitive failure, for example. We nourish the illusion that everyone can win the race if they have "the right stuff," so economic success becomes a measure of personal adequacy. Other political systems also make more effort to help those who succumb to drugs or alcohol. We see the modest success rates of such programs as evidence of their futility rather than evidence that they need to be improved.

The same both-and logic applies to the homeless mentally ill. Homelessness spread during the 1980s partly because states pushed a lot of very sick people out of hospitals without offering them anywhere else to live. The legislators who endorsed this policy have much to answer for. But that does not mean the mentally ill bear no responsibility for their fate. Only a small minority of the mentally ill ended up on the streets. This was partly because they had no family members willing to look after them and partly because their particular symptoms were more conducive to homelessness. But the mentally ill, like children, must still take some responsibility for their own actions and share some of the blame for the consequences. If they are not sane enough to do that, they really do need to live in hospitals.

Even in America, the world's most commercialized society, blame is still free. That means there is always plenty for everyone.

5. Jobs and Marriage

When homelessness first became a national issue during the early 1980s, many people blamed the problem on the economy, which was producing unemployment rates near 10 percent for the first time since the 1930s. When economic recovery failed to make a perceptible dent on homelessness, such explanations lost some of their appeal. But many Americans still attribute the spread of homelessness to the dearth of job opportunities for unskilled workers.[1] In addition, some think cutbacks in government benefits have made it harder for people without jobs to keep a roof over their heads.

Changes in the labor market could also have contributed to rising homelessness among women, but hardly anyone makes that argument. Instead, most observers blame the spread of homelessness among women on the decline of marriage, which left more women fending for themselves. The fact that fewer women have husbands seems particularly likely to have pushed up homelessness among children, since men seldom do much to support their children unless they live under the same roof, and unskilled women can seldom support themselves and their children on their earnings alone.

Any given individual's chances of being homeless obviously fall on a continuum that runs from very high to very low. If you have no salable skills, no claim to government benefits, no friends or relatives willing to help out, and spend whatever money you have on crack, you are likely to become homeless. If you have skills that employers value, unemployment compensation when you lose your job, an extended family with a commitment to helping one another, and a strong aversion to drugs and alcohol, your chances of ending up homeless are negligible.

If we knew the exact impact of the diverse personal and social considerations that influence an individual's chances of ending up homeless, we could develop a "vulnerability index" based on the odds that individuals with different traits would be homeless on a given night. Then we could trace the number of people with high vulnerability scores over time and see whether the change was sufficient to explain the increase in homelessness. No such index exists, but Peter Rossi has suggested a strategy for creating a useful first approximation.[2]

Martha Burt's 1987 survey of shelters, soup kitchens, and congregating sites in large cities found that the homeless had four economically notable characteristics: 97 percent were too young to qualify for old-age assistance; 97 percent had no spouse to help them out; 94 percent had no steady job; and 80 percent of those without children had cash incomes below $250 during the month before the survey.[3]

These facts suggest that the group most vulnerable to homelessness is composed of unmarried working-age adults in conventional housing who have no earnings and extremely low personal incomes. When estimating the size of this group I include everyone between the ages of twenty-one and sixty-four who was not living with a spouse, did no paid work during the previous calendar year, and had a total personal income below $2500 a year.[4] (Here and throughout this book, all incomes, rents, and other prices are in 1989 dollars unless I indicate otherwise.)

In order to keep the story simple, I focus on three business-cycle peaks: 1969, 1979, and 1989.[5] In 1969 the Vietnam boom was cresting, only 3.4 percent of the labor force was unemployed, and hardly anyone worried about homelessness. In 1979 the nation had suffered through five years of slow growth and rapid inflation, 5.8 percent of the labor force was unemployed, and homelessness was just emerging as a public issue. In 1989 the economy had finally recovered from the deep recession of the early 1980s, 5.2 percent of the labor force was unemployed, and the homeless were everywhere.

Table 5. Percent of Household Members Aged 21 to 64 Who Did No Paid Work, Reported Incomes below $2500, or Did Not Live with a Spouse, 1969, 1979, and 1989

	Men			Women		
Characteristic	1969	1979	1989	1969	1979	1989
No earnings[a]	5.3%	8.1%	9.9%	41.2%	32.8%	26.9%
Unmarried	20.3	29.9	36.9	23.9	31.7	36.8
Personal income below $2500	4.1	4.3	5.8	47.3	30.9	22.1
Personal income below $2500 and no earnings	1.7	2.2	3.4	36.3	23.1	16.8
Personal income below $2500 and unmarried	2.6	2.7	3.8	4.0	3.4	4.1
Personal income below $2500, unmarried, and no earnings	1.2	1.5	2.4	2.6	2.3	2.8
Personal income below $2500, unmarried, and living with own children	—[b]	—[b]	.1	.6	.8	1.2
Personal income below $2500, living with own children and no other adult	—[b]	—[b]	.1	.3	.4	.8

Source: Bureau of the Census, March Current Population Survey. Living arrangements are for March 1970, 1980, and 1990. Incomes are converted to 1989 dollars using the 1982–83 fixed-weight price index for personal consumption expenditures from the national income and product accounts.

a. No paid employment during the calendar year.

b. Less than .05.

Long-Term Joblessness among Men

Table 5 shows that the proportion of working-age men who reported no paid work for a full calendar year rose from 5 percent in 1969 to 8 percent in 1979 and 10 percent in 1989. This was not just a matter of more men taking early retirement. Long-term joblessness also increased among men between the ages of twenty-five and forty-four. (Men under the age of twenty-five had higher rates of short-term joblessness, but

the proportion who went a full year without working was no higher in
the late 1980s than in the late 1960s.[6])

There is no consensus about why long-term joblessness increased
among mature men. Most of the increase occurred well before crack
hit the streets. Deinstitutionalization of the mentally ill must have played
some role, because the unemployable mentally ill are more likely to
show up in household surveys today than in the past. But this change
could not have driven up long-term male joblessness by more than one
percentage point, and its effect was probably far less than that.

Many Americans blame increased joblessness on the decline of the
work ethic. I do not know whether the proportion of Americans who
feel that work is intrinsically virtuous has changed over the past generation, but long-term joblessness did not increase much during the
1960s, when antiwork sentiments were stronger than at any time in
recent memory. Long-term joblessness began to climb during the
1970s, and the trend continued during the 1980s, when almost everyone gave at least lip service to the work ethic. Nor can one argue that
the 1960s just had a delayed effect on the baby-boom generation. When
long-term joblessness began to climb in the 1970s, it affected men of
all ages, including those who were already "thirty something" during the
cultural upheavals of the 1960s.[7]

A somewhat different cultural theory holds that long-term joblessness increased because fewer men got married. According to this view,
men work regularly at unrewarding jobs only if the people with whom
they live depend on their earnings to make ends meet. Marriage rates
declined precipitously during the 1970s and 1980s (see Table 5). That
could have reduced the pressure on men to maximize their income,
making them choosier about the jobs they would take. In reality,
however, long-term joblessness increased fastest among married men.[8]
This suggests—though it does not prove—that increased employment
among wives may have made husbands choosier about the jobs they
would accept.

Changes in the economy may also have pushed more men out of
the labor force, but it is not clear how this happened. The trend cannot
be blamed mainly on slack labor markets, because short-term joblessness did not increase much among prime-age men during this period.[9]
It is true that unskilled workers' real wages declined during this period,

which could have led more men to drop out of the labor market.[10] But unskilled men's real wages were no lower in the late 1980s than in the late 1950s, when far more of them worked.

It is clear that the demand for unskilled workers fell faster than the supply of such workers during the late 1970s and 1980s. This change probably had two distinct effects. First, unskilled workers' relative wages fell. Second, the least desirable workers had trouble finding work at any wage. Declining demand for day laborers may have been particularly important for these men. Although steady work usually helps stabilize people's lives, some alcoholics and schizophrenics are likely to do better in a labor market that allows them to work on their good days while staying in bed on their bad days. If they can pick up a day's work by showing up on a streetcorner early in the morning, they can earn something almost every week. If they have to be at work every day, they lose their job. I know no statistics on the demand for day laborers, but many observers think it has declined sharply and that such demand as still exists is mostly met by immigrants. If so, that would help explain why America's least reliable native-born workers so often have no work.

The Safety Net for Men

When a man does not work, he can stay off the street in one of three ways. If he has substantial savings or inherited wealth, he can live off this money. If he is entitled to significant government benefits or a private pension, that too can keep him housed. Finally, if his own income is inadequate, he may be able to get help from relatives or friends. When I speak of a safety net, I mean the combined effect of these three sources of security.

Changes in jobless men's personal income are easier to measure than changes in their ability to make claims on others. The proportion of all long-term jobless males reporting extremely low personal incomes declined from 31 percent in 1969 to 27 percent in 1979, suggesting that the safety net improved somewhat. By 1989 the figure had climbed back to 34 percent, suggesting that the holes in the safety net had grown.[11] But the changes are all small, so the basic story is one of stability, not change.

One should not take these figures too literally. Census respondents generally underreport income from dividends, interest, rent, unemploy-ment insurance, disability benefits, and public assistance. Since these are the principal sources of personal income available to the long-term jobless, some of the men who reported incomes below $2500 probably had more than that.[12] But there is no evidence that income of this kind is less fully reported today than in the past. That means the holes in the economic safety net were probably as large in 1989 as in 1969, even though their exact size remains uncertain.

When long-term joblessness is rising, the number of people falling through the safety net will increase unless the holes get smaller. Since the holes were no smaller in 1989 than in 1969, the proportion of all working-age males with extremely low incomes rose (from 4.1 percent in 1969 to 5.8 percent in 1989—see Table 5). The increase was entirely accounted for by the fact that fewer working-age men had any earnings at all.

Even if a working-age man has very little income of his own, he can usually stay off the street if he can stay married, because his wife can keep the whole family afloat. The value of marriage for men should not be exaggerated, however. A young man who cannot hold a job has trouble finding a wife, and an older married man who cannot hold a job often loses his wife. Only an intact marriage protects men from homelessness, and the same forces that leave men jobless often leave them single as well.

Table 5 shows that marriage rates declined precipitously between 1969 and 1989. Had this also happened among men with extremely low incomes, the number of men vulnerable to homelessness would have grown even faster than the number with extremely low incomes. In reality, however, marriage rates did not change much among working-age men with extremely low incomes: 35 percent were married in 1969, 37 percent in 1979, and 33 percent in 1989. Marriage rates declined sharply only among more affluent men. Much of the decline occurred among men who also worked full time throughout the year.[13]

Because neither marriage rates nor the chances of ending up with an extremely low income changed much among the long-term jobless between 1969 and 1989, the overall proportion of men vulnerable to homelessness rose far less than one might have expected. The proportion of working-age men with no spouse and personal income below $2500 hardly changed during the 1970s, and it only rose from 2.7 to 3.8 percent during the 1980s (see Table 5). If we concentrate on the most vulnerable group of all—those who had no spouse, extremely low income, and no earnings—this group went from 1.5 percent of all working-age men in 1979 to 2.4 percent in 1989. These trends surely explain some of the increase in homelessness, but they are nothing like large enough to explain the entire problem. The prevalence of homelessness among those at greatest risk must also have increased.

The Decline of Marriage among Women

While long-term joblessness increased among men, the story was very different for women. The proportion of working-age women without any earnings fell from 41 percent in 1969 to 27 percent in 1989. The proportion with extremely low incomes fell even more (see Table 5). Had women's chances of becoming homeless depended entirely on their own income, therefore, the number of homeless women would have declined sharply during these years.

But while women's personal incomes were rising, their other main source of economic support, namely marriage, was in decline. Women married later, divorced more often, and were less likely to remarry. In contrast to the pattern among men, moreover, marriage declined even among women with extremely low personal incomes. In 1969, 91 percent of women with extremely low personal incomes were married. By 1979 the figure was 89 percent, and by 1989 it was down to 82 percent. As a result, the proportion of working-age women with neither a spouse nor enough money of their own to keep off the street shows no clear trend over time, falling from 4.0 percent in 1969 to 3.4 percent in 1979 but then rising to 4.1 percent in 1989. Thus if nothing else had changed, we would have expected a small decline in homelessness among unmarried women during the 1970s, followed by a small increase during the 1980s.

But a third major change was also occurring: more unmarried women with extremely low incomes had children. In 1969 only 16 percent of all unmarried working-age women with extremely low personal incomes had a child. By 1979 the figure was 23 percent, and by 1989 it was 31 percent.[14] The effect of this change was accentuated by the fact that more poor single mothers were living on their own. In both 1969 and 1979 half of all single mothers with personal income below $2500 were living with at least one other adult. By 1989 the proportion was down to 36 percent.[15]

None of these figures should be taken too literally. No urban family, no matter how frugal, can survive for an entire year on $2500 worth of goods and services. Single mothers who report household incomes that low must have access to additional resources of some kind in order to survive. Many get food stamps and free medical care. Some also get housing subsidies. Many have off-the-books jobs or an unreported boyfriend who helps pay the bills.[16] But even when families that report incomes below $2500 are not going hungry, their economic situation is often precarious. If the mother's boyfriend moves out, if her off-the-books job vanishes, or if the father of her children stops giving her $100 a month because he has gone to jail, the family can find itself on the street.

Income statistics also exaggerate the decline in single mothers' living standards since 1969, because fewer government benefits for such women come in cash. Cash benefits rose from 1965 to 1974 but lagged behind inflation after that.[17] Noncash benefits have grown fairly steadily since 1965, although the rate of growth slowed after 1980. Medicaid, passed in 1965, provided welfare mothers with free health care. Food stamps, which grew dramatically during the 1970s, now pay a substantial fraction of their grocery bills. Low-income housing programs, which have also grown steadily since the early 1970s, now help a significant minority of single mothers pay their rent.

Although noncash benefits continued to grow after 1980, this growth does not distort trend estimates for extreme poverty to the same extent during the 1980s as during the 1970s. The cost of Medicaid grew rapidly, but this did nothing to help single mothers pay their other bills. The number of single mothers getting federal housing subsidies also grew, but even in 1990 only a quarter of welfare recipients got such a subsidy.[18] As a result, the post-1980 decline in welfare recipients' income is likely to be real.

Like the increase in long-term joblessness among men, the decline of marriage among couples with children is controversial and poorly understood. Taken one at a time, economic explanations raise as many questions as they answer. Some have argued, for example, that marriage declined during the 1970s and 1980s because unskilled men's real wages fell, making it harder for a man to support a family.[19] But marriage rates declined almost as fast among men with good jobs as among men generally, which is precisely the opposite of what we would expect if the demand for affluent husbands had remained constant while the supply dwindled. Others have argued that marriage declined because job opportunities for women improved during the 1970s and 1980s, allowing them to be choosier about the men they would marry.[20] But that cannot explain why more women without jobs remained unmarried. Nor can we blame the latter trend on increased welfare benefits, since the purchasing power of the welfare package declined during the 1980s.

If we assume that the marriage market is highly stratified by education, labor-market changes provide a more plausible explanation for what happened. Highly educated women may have become much choosier about the men they would marry because they found it easier to support themselves without a man's help. Rather than marrying less-educated women, highly educated men may have responded to this change by remaining single. Meanwhile, poorly educated women may have lost interest in marriage because the men available to them were also poorly educated, and these men had become less able to support a family. Poorly educated men may then have remained single because they had no choice, or because they did not want to marry unless they could enjoy the psychological benefits of being their family's sole breadwinner.

Changes in sexual norms have also reduced the appeal of marriage. Thirty years ago few communities tolerated regular, open sexual relationships between unmarried partners. Today most communities do so. In those places that still support traditional sexual norms, marriage rates remain relatively high despite the fact that women's earning power has risen faster than men's.

Marriage may also have lost its appeal partly because of growing disagreement about the proper division of labor between husbands and wives. Many people imagine that this change is confined to the college-educated, who are more likely to have been touched by self-conscious feminism. But the war between the sexes is at least as intense among high-school dropouts as among college graduates, even though it is less often couched in ideological terms.[21] The groups in which marriage remains most common are those in which women remain relatively subservient.

Whatever its causes, the decline of marriage has played a major role in the spread of homelessness among women and children. Yet as we have seen, the decline of marriage would not in itself have driven up homelessness very much. It was the fact that unskilled women not only married less but continued to have children that pushed more of them into the streets.

Recession and Recovery

Although the number of people who were economically vulnerable grew during the 1980s, it did not grow steadily. As one would expect, the number surged during the early 1980s, when the economy went into deep recession. Unemployment began to fall in 1984. This decline did not appreciably reduce the number of jobless adults with very low incomes, but it did keep the number from growing. Table 6 illustrates this pattern. All the groups most vulnerable to homelessness grew rapidly between 1979 and 1984. Few grew much between 1984 and 1989, and some actually contracted. I do not yet have comparable data for the early 1990s, but I would be astonished if these groups had not grown again after the recession began in 1990.

If we compare the size of these high-risk groups to the number of people who were actually homeless, a puzzle emerges. High-risk groups grew as fast as the homeless population in the early 1980s, suggesting that homelessness was simply a byproduct of extreme poverty. But homelessness continued to spread in the late 1980s, when the groups at greatest risk were no longer growing. The puzzle is especially clear for childless adults. We must therefore think of homelessness as having spread in two distinct phases. During the early 1980s, the economically vulnerable population grew while the odds that its members would become homeless remained relatively constant. During the late 1980s, the economically vulnerable population grew far less, but the odds that its members would become homeless rose.

Table 6. Number of Persons and Families at Risk of Becoming Homeless and Actually Homeless, 1969, 1979, 1984, and 1989

	Number (thousands)				Pct. increase	
Group	1969	1979	1984	1989	1979–84	1984–89
PERSONS AGED 21 TO 64						
Homeless	na	121	201	312	66%	55%
Household members with income below $2500 and no spouse						
Men	1250	1570	3050	2640	94	−13
Women	2110	2080	2950	2930	42	−1
Household members with income below $2500, no spouse, and no earnings						
Men	570	860	1640	1600	91	−2
Women	1340	1430	1910	2010	34	5
FAMILIES WITH CHILDREN						
Homeless	<1	<1	4	20	>300	400
Unmarried mothers aged 21 to 64 in households						
Income below $2500[a]	330	480	850	900	77	6
Income below $2500 and no other adult in household[b]	152	235	361	579	54	60
Income below $5000 and no other adult in household[b]	359	604	1024	1439	70	41

Source: Household population from March Current Population Survey, with estimates rounded to nearest 10,000. Homeless population estimated from Table 2 by assuming that 1979 was the same as 1980, that 1989 was midway between March, 1988 and March, 1990, that 3 percent of the homeless were over the age of sixty-five in all years, and that homeless families averaged 1.1 adults and 2.2 children in all years.

a. Includes mothers who head subfamilies.

b. Household includes no one over the age of eighteen except the head.

The risk that economically vulnerable individuals will become homeless could have risen after 1984 for at least four reasons. First, as I suggested in the previous chapter, the crack epidemic could have diverted some rent money to other uses. Second, rents could have risen faster than the general level of inflation, making it harder for people to find affordable shelter even when their overall purchasing power was constant. I examine this possibility in the next chapter and return to it in Chapter 8. Third, the decline of marriage may have been linked to a general weakening of family ties that left more of the very poor without relatives willing to help them (see Chapter 7). Fourth, as more communities opened shelters, more of the people who were doubled up in high-stress situations may have chosen to move to these shelters (see Chapter 10).

6. The Destruction of Skid Row

Soon after homelessness emerged as a national problem in the early 1980s, a small but influential group of housing advocates began arguing that changes in the housing market had played a major role in creating the problem. They told two stories. The first, which I discuss in this chapter, tried to explain why single adults who once lived in skid-row hotels now live in shelters and bus stations. The villains of this drama were the politicians and planners who let developers replace "single room occupancy" (SRO) hotels and rooming houses with shopping malls, office buildings, and up-scale apartments. The housing advocates' second story, which I discuss in Chapter 8, tried to explain why more families with children were showing up in shelters. This account emphasized the growing shortage of what advocates called "affordable" housing for families.

How Many SRO Rooms Were Lost?

Almost everyone who tries to explain the spread of homelessness mentions the destruction of SROs, but hardly anyone says precisely what an SRO is. This ambiguity seems to reflect the bureaucratic origins of the term. Over the past century most cities have adopted increasingly stringent rules about the kinds of housing developers can put up. In most cases these rules apply only to new units. Existing units are usually exempt under some kind of grandfather clause. The term SRO typically describes older buildings divided into single rooms that do not meet a city's current standards for new construction.

Because building codes vary from city to city and are constantly changing, what gets counted as an SRO varies both from place to place and over time. Indeed, different agencies in the same city sometimes define an SRO differently. In one case it may be a cubicle hotel in which the rooms have no windows or have less than 60 square feet of floorspace. In another case it may be any hotel or rooming house in which the rooms do not have their own bathroom. In a third case the term may cover all one-room units without their own bathroom and kitchen.

If we want to understand what happened to the supply of one-room rental units, we need to impose some order on this chaos. The simplest approach is to use Census data to trace changes in the number of one-room rental units with different characteristics. Three kinds of rooms seem especially relevant to the problems of the poor: rooms without kitchens, rooms without bathrooms, and rooms in hotels and rooming houses. Cheap hotels and rooming houses are important because they usually rent by the day or the week as well as the month, and few demand security deposits.

The Census Bureau's American Housing Survey (AHS), which began in 1973, provides the best available data on one-room rental units, but it has three important limitations.[1] First, it does not survey many one-room units in any given year.[2] Second, it does not cover tenants in hotels patronized mainly by transients unless they have been there—or expect to be there—for at least six months. Third, the AHS changed the way it counted rooms in 1985. From 1973 through 1983 the AHS let tenants decide for themselves how many rooms they had.[3] If an apartment had a main room plus a kitchen set into an alcove, for example, the tenant could say the apartment had either one or two rooms. Starting in 1985, the AHS began asking respondents whether their home had specific kinds of rooms, such as a living room, a dining room, a bedroom, a kitchen, and so on. As a result of this change, a quarter of the nation's one-room units became two-room units.

Most discussions of rented rooms concentrate on what the Census Bureau calls dwelling units, and I do the same in this chapter. A room constitutes a separate dwelling unit only if a tenant can reach it directly

Table 7. Number of One-Room Rental Units with Various Characteristics, 1973–1989

(Numbers in thousands)

	Old room definition			New room definition		Net change	
						1973–	1985–
Characteristic	1973	1979	1983	1985	1989	83	89
Total	1114	1134	1134	816	789	+20	−27
Occupied units	920	991	981	713	672	+61	−41
In hotel or rooming house[a]	314	221	171	116	162	−143	46
No complete bathroom	328	233	236	155	175	−92	20
No complete kitchen	442	306	298	256	238	−144	−18

Source: Tabulations by David Rhodes from the American Housing Survey.

a. Covers rooms in rooming houses and nontransient hotels, plus rooms in transient hotels occupied by the same person for six months or more.

from the street or from a common hall. If a tenant has to walk through someone else's home to reach a room, it is not a separate dwelling unit and the tenant is counted as a member of the household in which the room is located. (I discuss people who rent such rooms later.)

Table 7 shows that the AHS count of one-room rental units hardly changed from 1973 to 1983, hovering around 1.1 million. When the AHS was redesigned in 1985, the count fell to around 800,000.[4] After that, the count remained stable through 1989. Since there was no decline in the number of one-room rental units between 1973 and 1983 or between 1985 and 1989, the apparent decline between 1983 and 1985 is almost certainly a byproduct of the change in survey design (or in the sample).[5] The decennial Census confirms this judgment. The 1990 Census let tenants decide for themselves what counted as a room and found 1.2 million occupied one-room units, which was only 100,000 fewer than the 1970 and 1980 Censuses had found using the same question (see Appendix Table A.2).

While the total number of one-room units was essentially stable from 1973 to 1989, the number of people living in hotels and rooming houses declined from 314,000 in 1973 to 171,000 in 1983. There was another sharp decline between 1983 and 1985. Because this simply continues the earlier downward trend, and because very few rooms in hotels or rooming houses have their own kitchen, I assume this drop was real. The decline was reversed after 1985, however, and the 1989 count was almost as high as that for 1983.[6] Taken at face value, the AHS suggests that the number of people living in hotels and rooming houses fell by about 90,000 between 1973 and 1979, and by about 60,000 during the 1980s.

The decennial Census tells roughly the same story. The Census found 640,000 people with no other permanent address in hotels and rooming houses in 1960. The figure was down to 320,000 in 1970 and 204,000 in 1980. The exact 1990 figure is uncertain, but it was on the order of 137,000 (see Appendix Table A.2). The Census therefore implies that the number of hotel residents fell by 120,000 during the 1970s and 60,000 during the 1980s, which is consistent with the AHS.

The number of one-room rental units without a kitchen or a complete bathroom declined at roughly the same rate as the number of rooms in hotels and rooming houses.[7] If we concentrate on the years between 1979 and 1989, Table 7 shows that the number of occupied one-room units without complete bathrooms declined by 58,000, while the number without complete kitchens declined by 68,000. The changes between 1973 and 1979 are much larger, but blaming the destruction of SROs in the 1970s for increases in homelessness a decade later raises obvious problems.

Those who believe that tearing down SROs played a major role in the spread of homelessness usually claim that far more than 60,000 rooms were lost. Indeed, the most widely cited estimate is that 1.1 million rooms were lost between 1970 and 1982. More than 100,000 rooms are often said to have been lost in New York City alone.[8] Losses of 10,000 or more rooms have been reported in a number of other large cities.[9] These estimates differ from mine in two important respects. First, the biggest numbers—notably the nationwide decline of 1.1 million units—come from a study that included two-room apartments. Second, the big losses all occurred during the 1970s rather than the 1980s.

Treating the disappearance of SRO rooms during the 1960s and 1970s as a cause of increased homelessness during the 1980s poses the same logical problem we encountered with deinstitutionalization. How, the skeptic must ask, could tearing down SROs during the 1960s or 1970s drive up homelessness ten or twenty years later? Where were the former SRO residents living in the meantime? If they found alternative housing when the old SROs vanished, what happened in the 1980s to make them homeless? I think all these questions have logical answers, but the answers transform our understanding of the whole process in a fundamental way.

Price Changes

Most of the old SROs were torn down during the 1960s and early 1970s, when both real wages and government benefits were rising. Because real wages were going up, even irregularly employed single adults were increasingly able to afford a room with a bathroom and kitchen. Because a growing proportion of the aged and disabled were eligible for federal benefits and these benefits were becoming more generous, they too could afford better accommodations. Noting this, most people who wrote about SROs in the 1960s and 1970s assumed they would all be gone within a couple of decades.

After 1974 both real wages and government benefits stopped rising, so demand for SRO rooms probably stopped falling. But because there was still a lot of excess capacity in the SRO system, prices did not rise and the process of destruction continued. As far as I can tell, no general shortage of cheap rooms developed until around 1980, when the number of extremely poor single adults began to climb.[10] (In this as in everything else, New York City was apparently an exception.)

The evidence available to document this argument is far from ideal. The decennial Census has never asked people who live in hotels or rooming houses how much rent they pay, so we have no systematic data on rent levels in these places before 1973, when the AHS began. The AHS sample is quite small; it does not cover most people in transient hotels; and it cannot tell us anything reliable about what happened between 1983 and 1985.

For simplicity, I compare changes in the number of very cheap rooms to changes in the number of very poor tenants who lived in a single room. I call rooms very cheap when the tenant's rent and utility bills ("gross rent") came to less than $150 a month in 1989 dollars. I call tenants very poor when their personal income was less than 80 percent of the federal poverty line for a single individual. This puts my cutoff at $5000 in 1989.

Figure 2 shows that there were 178,000 very poor tenants and 265,000 very cheap rooms in 1973. Both numbers rose dramatically between 1973 and 1975. That was not because rents or incomes fell. Rather, the jump in oil prices after the 1973–74 embargo drove up prices in most sectors of the American economy much sooner than it drove up rents or incomes. As a result, "real" rents and incomes both fell. But the balance between the supply of very cheap rooms and the incomes of the people likely to live in them does not appear to have changed much.

Although inflation continued through the rest of the 1970s, Figure 2 suggests that the balance between supply and demand remained fairly stable. There were 87,000 more very cheap rooms than very poor tenants in 1973. In 1981 the difference was 84,000. Other measures also suggest that the supply of cheap rooms kept pace with demand. The

Figure 2. Changes in the Number of Very Low Rent Rooms and Very Low Income Tenants Living in One-Room Units, 1973–1989

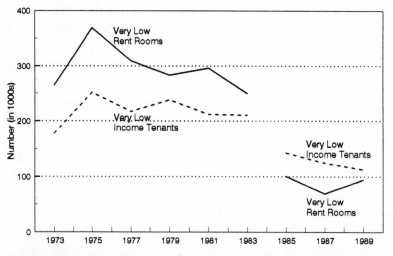

Source: American Housing Survey. Very low rent rooms cost less than $150 per month (1989 dollars) for rent and utilities. Very low income tenants are those in one-room units with annual income below $5000 per year (1989 dollars).

median rent for a single room was 33 percent of the median tenant's income in both 1973 and 1981, for example.

After 1981 both the housing situation and the data describing it took a marked turn for the worse. The AHS recorded a 15 percent decline in the number of very cheap rooms between 1981 and 1983, while the number of very poor tenants remained constant. As a result, the median rent for a single room jumped from 33 to 40 percent of the median tenant's income. What happened between 1983 and 1985 is anybody's guess. The revamped AHS counted only 101,000 very cheap rooms in 1985, down from 250,000 in 1983. Part of this decline was a byproduct of the Census Bureau's new approach to counting rooms, which cut the total number of one-room units by 28 percent. But the proportion of single rooms costing less than $150 also fell from 26 percent in 1983 to 15 percent in 1985, which is by far the biggest two-year change recorded in the AHS. Some of this decline was undoubtedly real, but some of it may have been a byproduct of changes in the survey.

The number of very poor tenants in one-room units also fell between 1983 and 1985, but far less than the estimated number of very cheap rooms. After 1985, therefore, very poor tenants were more numerous than very cheap rooms. Figure 2 suggests that this situation may have improved a little between 1985 and 1989, but given the small number of cases it is hard to be sure.[11]

My best guess, then, is that a modest decline in the supply of cheap rooms interacted with a significant increase in potential demand to drive up room rents much faster than the general price level. The increase in demand was, in turn, driven by the forces described in the previous chapter: increases in long-term male joblessness and lagging government benefits for those without jobs.

We can test this claim by tracing changes in mean rent for unsubsidized rooms of constant quality. If we convert rent and utility charges to 1989 dollars, the observed mean for all unsubsidized rooms rises from $225 a month in 1973 to $332 in 1989. Part of this increase is traceable to the fact that single rooms were increasingly likely to have their own bathroom, their own kitchen, and other amenities. To control for the effect of these changes, Figure 3 shows trends in what I will call "quality-adjusted" rent. This is what tenants paid in different years for rooms with the characteristics of the rooms they rented in 1973. For comparison, Figure 3 also shows the quality-adjusted mean for all rental units, regardless of size.[12]

Once we adjust for qualitative improvements, mean rents for unsubsidized one-room units remain virtually constant during the 1970s. This is consistent with my argument that the destruction of cheap SRO rooms during the 1970s was a response to weak demand. After 1979, quality-adjusted rents rise quite rapidly, even after adjusting for the general level of inflation. As we have seen, the number of low-quality rooms did not decline much after 1979. The price increases shown in Figure 3 must therefore have been driven primarily by rising demand rather than falling supply. This judgment is reinforced by comparing quality-adjusted rents for one-room units to those for the rental market as a whole. Quality-adjusted rents for one-room units rose less than those for the market as a whole during the 1970s. After 1979 this pattern was reversed, with quality-adjusted rents rising faster for one-room units than for the market as a whole.

These data all suggest that a shortage of SRO rooms developed in the early 1980s. That change probably contributed to the increase in

Figure 3. Mean Monthly Rents in 1989 Dollars for Unsubsidized Units of Constant Quality, 1973–1989

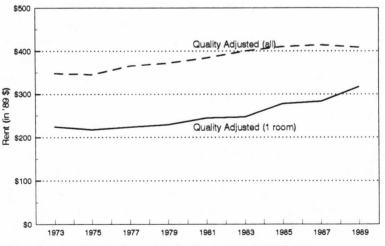

Source: American Housing Survey. For details see Appendix Table A.3.

homelessness after 1981. But the shortage appears to have been created largely by rising demand and only secondarily by falling supply.

How Could the Homeless Afford SROs?

Those who think the destruction of SROs played a major role in the spread of homelessness must also solve another puzzle. Although SRO residents are extremely poor by mainstream American standards, few were ever as poor as most of today's homeless. Four fifths of all homeless single adults took in less than $2500 in cash during 1987. Only 100,000 people that poor were living in single rooms during the 1970s. Since nearly 50,000 people that poor were still living in single rooms in the late 1980s, only 50,000 appear to have been pushed out of one-room units. That could explain part of the increase in homelessness after 1979, but not a large part.[13]

Another way to assess the likely impact of tearing down the old SROs is to ask what might happen if they were rebuilt. Suppose HUD were to rebuild all the SROs torn down between 1975 and 1985 and rent them for what they cost in 1975, adjusted upward for general inflation. Roughly speaking, that would mean creating 150,000 rooms of extremely low quality and renting them for an average of $150 a month. (The figure would obviously be higher in cities like New York and Los Angeles, lower in cities like Omaha and Memphis.)

Advocacy groups seldom suggest that rooms costing $150 a month would get many of the homeless off the streets, but that may not prove much. Most advocates are committed to the principle that nobody should have to spend more than 30 percent of their income on rent—a doctrine rooted in the fact the federal government sets subsidized rents at 30 percent of the tenant's income. By this standard people need an income of $500 a month before they can afford a room costing $150. Less than 5 percent of the homeless single adults who used big-city shelters and soup kitchens in 1987 reported incomes that high.

In reality, however, nearly two fifths of the nation's tenants currently spend more than 30 percent of their income on rent, and the proportion is even higher among the poor. What people are willing to spend on rent depends not on what Congress deems reasonable but on how much they value shelter relative to other things, and how adept they are at getting other things free. If the big-city homeless have time, bus fare, and a modicum of experience, they can often get the bulk of their food, clothing, and medical care free. If they do not crave caffeine, nicotine, alcohol, or cocaine, they can in principle spend a very large fraction of their cash on rent. But they may prefer to get their shelter free and spend their meager income on food, clothing, transportation, and stimulants. People's choices are almost as variable when they can spend $10 a day as when they can spend $1000.

It is also important to bear in mind that for the poorest of the poor daily rents often matter more than monthly rents. A drug user who takes in $10 a day panhandling will not save his money until the end of the month to rent a room. Whether he rents a room will depend on how he assesses the tradeoff between cocaine and shelter on a particular night. Renting rooms by the night is considerably more expensive than renting by the month. A hotel that rents cubicles for $175 a month may charge $8 a night for the same space. The price differential reflects both the fact that rooms rented by the day are often vacant and the greater risk that people who pay by the day will vomit in the hall.

The 1980 Census found 28,000 people living in rooms costing less than $4 a night. Allowing for inflation, such rooms would cost about $7 a night today. Not many of today's homeless could pay more than that on a regular basis. The 1990 Census did not report the number of rooms renting for such prices. Everyone agrees that they were scarce, but if only 28,000 people lived in such rooms in 1980, one can hardly argue that their elimination made a major contribution to homelessness.

Why No More Cheap Hotels?

While the number of very cheap rooms destroyed after 1980 was quite small, the fact that we lost any cheap rooms at all during a period of rising homelessness requires explanation. When extreme poverty increases and more people turn to free shelters, one also expects more people to seek out cheap hotels and rooming houses, which provide more privacy and make less effort to regulate their patrons' behavior. The 1980 Census found slightly more people in cheap hotels and rooming houses than in shelters. The number of single adults in shelters rose by a factor of about five between 1980 and 1990. One would therefore expect the number living in cheap hotels to have risen at least fivefold. Instead, the number apparently declined.

Going back to the 1950s sharpens the puzzle. In 1958, eight times as many Chicago residents lived in cage hotels as in shelters (see Table 3). By 1986 there were something like three times as many people in Chicago's shelters as in its two remaining cage hotels. The physical differences between a cage hotel and a shelter had not changed much. Why, then, did cage hotels lose clients while shelters gained new ones?

The most obvious answer is price. Chicago's cage hotels charged 50 to 90 cents a night in 1958.[14] If monthly discounts were the same then as now, a man could have gotten a room for $12 to $20 a month. The minimum wage was $1 an hour, so it probably took between twelve and twenty hours of minimum-wage work each month to pay for a cubicle. By 1992 Chicago had only one cage hotel with a listed telephone (the Wilson Men's Club Hotel). It charged $7.50 a night (or $162 a month). Similar places in New York, where they are officially called lodging houses, charged about the same amount.[15] The minimum wage was $4.25 an hour, so paying for a cubicle required forty hours of minimum-wage work a month instead of twelve to twenty.

I do not know how much the Wilson Hotel charged in 1958, but even if it was then a "top of the line" cage hotel charging 90 cents a night, its prices have risen by a factor of more than eight. The price of alcohol rose by a factor of less than three during this same period.[16] A six-pack of beer cost more than a cubicle in 1958, making privacy cheaper than oblivion. By 1992 a six-pack cost less than half as much as a cubicle, making oblivion cheaper than privacy. Price changes of this kind surely encourage the poor to spend more on booze and less on shelter. The same pattern holds if we compare the price of a cubicle to the price of cocaine.

There are two logically possible explanations for the rapid increase in cubicle prices: higher costs and higher profits. One way to estimate cost changes is to look at rents for conventional housing, which are generally set in a highly competitive market with many buyers and sellers. Rent increases in this market are likely to be roughly proportional to cost increases, at least over the long run. Rents for one-room apartments rose by a factor of eight between 1960 and 1989.[17] If landlords' costs also rose by a factor of roughly eight, cage hotels may not have significantly higher profit margins today than in the past.

This comparison is somewhat misleading, however, because Chicago's cage hotels do not seem to have improved their physical facilities since the 1950s, whereas most other one-room units have. In 1960, for example, only 30 percent of America's one-room rental units had a complete bathroom. By 1990, the figure was over 95 percent (see Appendix Table A.2). If the qualitative difference between a cage hotel and the average one-room dwelling widened, one would expect the cost differential to have widened as well.

Cage hotels' costs may, of course, have risen for reasons that had nothing to do with the quality of the service they offered. Increased violence and drug use may, for example, have forced these hotels to hire more staff. But drugs and violence have pushed up costs in all kinds of urban housing. Tenants have become more destructive, and they also demand more protection from outsiders.

The fact that rents rose at least as fast in cage hotels as in classier places may, then, be evidence that the market for cubicles was not functioning as textbooks say it should. Political considerations may have created an artificial shortage of cheap rooms, allowing the owners of the few remaining cage hotels to reap windfall profits.

In *New Homeless and Old* Charles Hoch and Robert Slayton describe how greed, politics, and ideology combined to destroy most of Chicago's cage hotels in the 1970s and early 1980s. These hotels were concentrated on West Madison Street just west of the Loop. In the 1960s developers began arguing that if the city would clear this neighborhood, they could fill it with up-scale housing that would keep affluent young people in the city and eventually repay the city's investment. The city agreed and began leveling the area in the late 1970s. The last cage hotels on West Madison were torn down in the early 1980s.

Because redevelopment eliminated so many cheap rooms so quickly, a temporary shortage was inevitable. But if this had been a textbook market, the story would not have ended there. Everything in Chicago is constantly being torn down, but almost everything that is profitable reappears somewhere else. If pulling down the cage hotels on West Madison had made the ones that survived elsewhere in the city more profitable, entrepreneurs should have created new ones. Many poor Chicago neighborhoods have vacant buildings that could easily be converted into cubicles. Had such conversions occurred, competition would have driven prices down again. Since that did not happen, we must ask why.

The simple answer is that entrepreneurs can no longer build cage hotels in Chicago because building-code requirements have changed. The same is true in most other cities. The nominal goal of these rules was to ensure that nobody would have to live in conditions as wretched as those in the old hotels, but I doubt that the issue was ever quite that simple. Even the dimmest Chicago alderman must have known that these rules would eventually mean higher rents, and that many skid-row residents could not afford such rents. Why, then, did they vote for such rules?

One way to answer this question is to ask who benefited from the new rules. The main beneficiaries were the owners of existing cheap hotels, who were allowed to remain in business and were protected from new competitors. The losers were the very poor, who had fewer housing options than before. Had the press described the costs and benefits of rules governing cheap hotels in these terms, Chicago politicians might have been reluctant to adopt them. But no one seems to have made arguments of this kind either in Chicago or elsewhere. Liberals who would ordinarily speak up for the very poor usually defended higher standards on the grounds that existing conditions were unconscionable. Perhaps they assumed that landlords would absorb the cost of improvements rather than passing them along to the poor, although it is hard to see why any sensible person would make such an extraordinary assumption.

Once homelessness became a major problem, cities like Chicago could have changed their rules, making it possible to create more rooms that the poor could afford. Few did so. Many decent people opposed such changes, on the grounds that private landlords should not be allowed to get rich renting rotten rooms to poor people. Most neighborhoods also supported restrictive rules, because they did not want anyone building a hotel nearby that would lure more deadbeats into their area.

Fifty years ago, when most cities still had an economically viable skid row, the restaurants, bars, and pawnshops in these areas prospered by catering to people who lived in nearby hotels. If an old hotel burned down, nearby businesses were eager to see it replaced, and the city was usually cooperative. Even the fire code was often bent to keep cheap hotels open. But once a city has redeveloped its skid row, creating a new one elsewhere is almost impossible. An entrepreneur who tries to create a flophouse will meet fierce opposition both from those who claim to have the interests of the poor at heart and from those who want the poor to live as far away as possible.

While tearing down cubicle hotels in the 1960s and 1970s did not make many people homeless at the time, I believe that the destruction of skid-row neighborhoods did make it harder to create housing for the very poor when their numbers began to grow again. Had cities been able to mothball skid rows during the affluent 1960s and 1970s the way the Navy mothballed old battleships, entrepreneurs could perhaps have created new cubicle hotels when demand revived in the 1980s. But once skid row was gone, it was hard to find any other area that viewed the very poor as a commercial asset rather than a liability. That fact, combined with changes in the laws about panhandling and vagrancy, encouraged destitute single adults to spread out over the entire city, turning every doorway into a potential flophouse.

Municipal policies that bar the creation of new cubicle hotels force the people who once patronized such places to live in shelters and public places. Yet a city that listens to its citizens has few alternatives. The very poor are a tiny minority, and they hardly ever vote. Citizens who want the poor to live as far away as possible are a large majority, and they vote regularly. That leaves the poorest of the poor with nowhere to go.

7. Social Skills and Family Ties

Although cubicle hotels were traditionally the cheapest form of shelter available to people who wanted to live alone, they never housed more than a small fraction of the nation's poor unmarried adults. Living alone has never been as cheap as living with other people, so most poor unmarried adults have always lived in someone else's home.

A room in a nonrelative's home cost about 20 percent less than a room in a hotel or rooming house in 1989. Partly for this reason, working-age adults were five times as likely to rent rooms in a nonrelative's household as in a hotel or rooming house.[1] Unfortunately, the Census Bureau did not collect data on roomers before 1985, and we do not know how either the number or the price of rented rooms in other people's homes has changed.

People who want to minimize their housing costs can save even more money if they find housemates and rent space together. Hotels and rooming houses charged an average of $283 a month in 1989, while rents averaged $392 a month in one-bedroom apartments, $476 in two-bedroom apartments, and $494 in three-bedroom apartments.[2] Thus if three typical SRO residents had rented a typical three-bedroom apartment, they could have cut their monthly rent from $849 to $494—a reduction of 42 percent. Living together in a three-bedroom apartment would also have provided them with more space per person, a bathroom shared with only two other people, a kitchen, and other amenities that are rare in hotels and rooming houses.

Who Shares Living Space?

Renting rooms is especially common in situations where potential landlords and tenants come from similar class backgrounds and have similar ideas about proper behavior. In college towns, for example, thousands of homeowners with grown children rent rooms to students. In immigrant communities, earlier immigrants who have accumulated a little capital often buy a home and rent rooms to more recent immigrants who resemble them in every respect but income.

When homeowners and their prospective tenants come from very different backgrounds, owners are often unwilling to rent out spare rooms even when they need the money. This is likely to be especially true if their prospective tenants hear voices, use crack, or think everyone is out to get them. Few homeowners want such people walking through their house every day.

Analogous problems arise when people look for roommates. Living with others requires a measure of social competence and willingness to compromise. If you have temper tantrums when you don't get your way, never clean up after you use the kitchen, or spend half the day intoxicated, your housemates will eventually ask for a divorce. After a few experiences of this kind, some people decide they need to live alone, even if that means paying more rent or settling for worse accommodations.

Despite the cost, 27 percent of all unmarried working-age adults lived alone in 1990. For most, living alone was a luxury. They valued their privacy and were willing to pay for it. For some, however, living alone was a necessity. Either they could not stand living with anyone else or no one else could stand living with them.

Because those who need to live alone must pay more for housing, they are more likely than other adults with comparable incomes to end up homeless. In 1987, a third of all the homeless adults who used services in large cities had lived alone just before becoming homeless. Almost all these individuals were both unmarried and nonelderly, and the great majority presumably had annual incomes below $5000 even before becoming homeless. Among people with these characteristics who lived in conventional housing, only 15 percent lived alone. Among those with incomes below $2500, only 10 percent lived alone.[3]

This comparison suggests that living alone doubles or triples an extremely poor unmarried adult's chances of becoming homeless. If we could track people over time, however, we would most likely find that living alone does not increase the odds of becoming homeless. My guess is that people who live alone are overrepresented among the homeless not because they are more likely to become homeless but because they stay homeless longer.

The socially adept homeless can often get off the streets very quickly, either by finding a job or by persuading a relative or lover to take them in until they find one. If they talk persuasively about giving up drink or drugs, they can often get someone to take them in without accumulating any cash at all. If they do not get a job or control their use of drugs or alcohol, their host may soon ask them to leave. But some people can repeat this cycle many times, mixing spells of homelessness with spells in conventional housing.

Loners, in contrast, can return to conventional housing only if they can save enough money to rent a place of their own. In the absence of outside help, they must usually pay several months' rent in advance to get their own place. That makes it almost impossible to get off the street unless they find steady work.

Are Family Ties Weakening?

Living with another adult not only reduces housing costs but helps create emotional ties that allow the indigent to make claims on the more affluent. As I noted earlier, married couples hardly ever become homeless as long as they stick together.[4] No one knows exactly how many people with spouses would be homeless if they were not married, but the number is surely sizable. In 1989, at the peak of the last business cycle, 1.2 million working-age husbands reported personal income below $2500. Some of these men were physically or mentally disabled. Some had no job for other reasons. Whatever the cause of their poverty, most relied on their wife's income to keep going. An even larger number of married women were probably one man away from homelessness.

When unmarried adults get into economic trouble, parents are usually their first line of defense against homelessness. In 1989, 5.6 million unmarried working-age adults had incomes below $2500. Forty-two percent of them lived with their parents, compared to only 9 percent of unmarried adults with incomes above $30,000. The contrast leaves little doubt that the main reason unmarried adults live with their parents is economic. It also shows how important parents are in keeping younger adults off the street, especially today when the income differential between the young and their elders is widening.

We have no systematic data on how much money adults who live with their parents contribute to their household's overall budget. Folklore suggests that they seldom pay their full share. Given their incomes, that seems inevitable in many cases. Some of these children are relatively young and will move out once they find steady work. Some have a physical or mental disability and will never be able to pay their way. Some have been self-sufficient in the past but have returned home because of a temporary setback.

Indigent adults who cannot live with a spouse or a parent often move in with some other relative. These individuals are as poor as those who live with their parents, so many cannot pay their fair share of the household's expenses. We have no data on the durability of these relationships. I suspect, however, that many are short-term. Most Americans are willing to take in relatives who have fallen on hard times if they think it will be a temporary arrangement until the individual "gets back on his feet." If that does not happen, tensions are likely to increase. When the host's patience runs out, the relationship is likely to end in mutual recrimination.

Families have traditionally been more willing to provide permanent support for indigent female relatives than for their indigent menfolk. Widows and maiden aunts often lived their entire life with more affluent kin, never paying their way. Today, however, most Americans expect a single woman to get a job. A woman who cannot hold a job may therefore be more vulnerable to homelessness than she was in an earlier era, especially if she becomes mentally ill or alcoholic after having lived alone or with a husband for an extended period.

Among unmarried adults who do not live with relatives, a growing minority live with sexual partners to whom they are not married. In 1990, 11 percent of all unmarried working-age adults reported that their household contained another unrelated adult of the opposite sex. This figure was up from 8 percent in 1980 and 3 percent in 1970.

Indirect evidence suggests that the true figures are even higher. In addition, an unknown but substantial number of gay couples share living quarters. Some of these nonmarital sexual partnerships involve people who would otherwise be homeless, but no one knows how many people stay off the street in this way.

These observations suggest that homelessness is likely to be inversely correlated with adults' inclination to live in groups. The number of working-age adults who were not married rose from 22 million in 1970 to 52 million in 1990. The number who were not living with any other adult rose just as rapidly, from 8 million in 1970 to 20 million in 1990.[5] Other things equal, these changes should have led to a steady increase in homelessness after 1970. Other things were not equal during the 1970s, because unmarried adults were becoming more affluent. After 1980, however, that pattern was reversed and the risks associated with living alone rose.

One popular explanation for homelessness is "family breakdown." In most cases that is just code for divorce and unwed parenthood. But if family ties are really loosening, we might expect fewer families to shelter their poor relations. I found little evidence of any such trend. The number of unmarried working-age adults with extremely low incomes (less than $2500) rose from 3.6 million in 1980 to 5.6 million in 1990—a huge increase. The fraction of this group living with relatives only fell from 58 to 55 percent. As a result, the fraction of all families sheltering such a relative rose substantially.

Families did not shelter *all* their down-at-heel relatives in 1990, but then they never have. Consider the mentally ill. Between 1955 and 1975 the proportion of the population living in state hospitals fell by three quarters.[6] Most of these individuals moved in with relatives. In these circumstances we can hardly charge today's families with doing less for their deranged kin than their parents or grandparents did. Quite the contrary. American families almost certainly shelter more of their mentally ill relatives today than at any time in living memory.

It is also true that the mentally ill are more likely to be on the streets. But that does not mean their relatives are more selfish than earlier generations of relatives were. The mentally ill often refuse to live with relatives. Even those who say they are willing to do so are often unwilling or unable to behave in ways that would allow their hosts to live anything remotely like a normal life. That was also the case in the nineteenth century, which was one reason legislators created mental hospitals.

The same logic applies to addicts. When crack arrived in the mid-1980s, poor men and women began using it. When people start using crack, they contribute less to the household budget, help out less with childcare, quarrel more with those around them, and often begin stealing from their housemates. The fact that today's families do not shelter all the nation's crack users is hardly evidence of growing selfishness. On the contrary, the fact that families still shelter most of these people shows that altruism is alive and well, even though it does not rule the world.

Nonetheless, we cannot afford to take this kind of family support for granted. Families have been getting smaller. Adults born in the 1950s typically have two or three living siblings to whom they can turn when they are in trouble. Most also grew up in two-adult households, giving them some claim on a number of aunts, uncles, and grandparents. Those now coming of age are more likely to have grown up with only one parent and one sibling. If their mother cannot help them and they do not get along with their sibling, they often have no claim on anyone else. As this situation becomes more common, kin may become a less useful source of emergency support.

8. Changes in the Housing Market

When we turn from the housing problems of single adults to those of families with children, we must broaden our focus to include larger rental units. The debate about homelessness then becomes enmeshed in an older and more general debate about low-income housing policy. This debate pits conservatives who think that government intrusion in the housing market is unnecessary against liberals who want the government to subsidize more low-income housing.

The central question in this debate has always been whether private entrepreneurs could provide low-income families with adequate housing at a price they could afford. Our answer to this question obviously depends on what kind of housing we judge adequate and how much we think any given family can afford. During the 1950s and 1960s, when housing prices were relatively stable, liberals based their calls for government intervention largely on the argument that poor people's housing was physically inadequate. These arguments buttressed the case for federal slum clearance and public housing projects. By the 1970s and 1980s, the physical quality of the housing stock had improved substantially, but rents were rising faster than incomes. Interventionists therefore shifted their emphasis from improving the physical quality of poor people's housing to lowering its price. This led to rent subsidies for low-income families.

In this chapter I begin by looking at how much rents increased during the 1970s and 1980s, and why that happened. Then I investigate the connection between rent increases and homelessness.

Changing Rent Burdens

The two best quantitative studies of homelessness are Peter Rossi's *Down and Out in America* and Martha Burt's *Over the Edge.* Both argue that during the 1970s and 1980s rents rose faster than poor tenants' ability to pay, and both suggest that this trend contributed to increased homelessness.[1] Most other discussions of homelessness make a similar argument.

Table 8 shows tenants' median income and rent in 1973, 1979, and 1989, which were the peaks of America's last three major business cycles. Once we adjust for inflation, the typical tenant's overall purchasing power hardly changed between 1973 and 1989.[2] But while tenants' purchasing power was flat, rent claimed a growing share of it: 27.1 percent in 1989 compared to 21.5 percent in 1973.[3] What housing analysts refer to as a tenant's "rent burden" therefore rose. This happened not because tenants' real income fell but because rents rose faster than the general level of inflation.

When we turn to low-income tenants, it is important to be clear whom we are talking about. The federal government's low-income housing programs are in principle open to all families with incomes below 80 percent of the median for their area. Using that standard, roughly 40 percent of all families are eligible. But when I talk about low-income tenants, I mean those with annual income below $10,000 (in 1989 dollars).[4] Only about a quarter of all tenants are currently that poor.

Low-income tenants spent a rising fraction of their income on rent during the 1970s and 1980s, just as the more affluent did. Once again, this was not because low-income tenants' purchasing power fell. Rather, the problem was that their rents rose faster than most other prices. As a result, the typical low-income tenant's rent burden climbed from 43.4 percent of income in 1973 to 51.6 percent in 1989.

Notice, though, that most of this increase occurred during the 1970s, before homelessness became a major issue. During the 1980s, low-income tenants' rent burden rose very little. That was because a growing proportion of low-income tenants got some kind of government rent subsidy.[5] If we look only at those low-income tenants who remained in unsubsidized housing, Table 8 shows that their rent burden rose almost as fast during the 1980s as during the 1970s.[6]

Table 8. Tenants' Monthly Income, Rent, and Vacancy Rates, 1973, 1979, and 1989

Income, rent, vacancy rate	1973	1979	1989	Percent change: 1973–89
ALL TENANTS				
Median monthly family income	$1512	$1395	$1500	−1%
Median monthly rent	$325	$352	$407	25
Rent burden[a]	21.5%	25.2%	27.1%	26
TENANTS WITH ANNUAL INCOME BELOW $10,000[b]				
Median monthly income	$506	$502	$495	−2
Median monthly rent	$219	$251	$256	17
Rent burden[a]	43.4%	50.0%	51.6%	19
Percent in subsidized units[c]	14.4%	21.2%	31.8%	121
TENANTS WITH ANNUAL INCOME BELOW $10,000 IN UNSUBSIDIZED UNITS				
Median monthly rent	$255	$296	$340	33
Rent burden[a]	49.5%	58.5%	68.1%	38
PERCENT OF UNSUBSIDIZED RENTAL UNITS VACANT				
Rent $250 or less a month[d]	7.7%	7.4%	9.0%	17
Rent above $250 a month[d]	8.3%	6.1%	8.7%	5
PRICE INDEX[e]	100	154	258	158

Source: American Housing Survey. Samples include tenants paying no cash rent. All rents include utility costs as well as contract rent. Family income is the combined income of the household head and all other household members related to the head by blood, marriage, or adoption. Utility costs were increased by 14 percent in 1989 to offset the effect of questionnaire changes.

a. Median rent as a percentage of median income.

b. Family income; excludes tenants reporting zero or negative income.

c. Includes both public housing and means-tested rent subsidies.

d. Contract rent.

e. Fixed-weight price index for personal consumption expenditure in 1982–83.

These facts convinced many people that low-income tenants faced a growing shortage of affordable housing. But if low-quality, low-rent housing had really been in short supply, the cheapest rental units should have had long waiting lists and low vacancy rates. Table 8 shows no such trend. Vacancy rates were slightly higher in unsubsidized low-rent units than in more expensive units throughout the late 1980s.[7] This pattern recurs when we focus on the East and West Coasts, where homelessness was most common. It also recurs when we look at metropolitan areas with more than a million residents. Persistently high vacancy rates in cheap housing have convinced most free-market enthusiasts that the alleged shortage of low-rent housing is a myth.[8]

Improvements in Quality

How are we to explain the fact that vacancy rates in low-rent housing remained high at a time when rent was rising faster than income? The simplest explanation is that rents rose because tenants no longer wanted to live in the kind of housing private landlords could provide for under $250 a month. Dissatisfied with what they could find at that price, tenants chose to pay more rent, even though that left them with less for everything else. Such a change in priorities could have had at least two sources: rising expectations about the physical quality of housing and growing aversion to bad neighborhoods.

The low-rent housing available in 1973 often lacked modern amenities, such as central heat and hot water. Many poor tenants who came of age before World War II saw these amenities as luxuries they could survive without. People who grew up after World War II were more likely to regard such amenities as necessities. The American Housing Survey shows that tenants at every income level were more likely to have complete bathrooms, complete kitchens, elevators, modern plumbing, central heat, and air conditioning in 1989 than in 1973. Tenants also had more rooms, even though their families were smaller. In most cases the improvement was biggest among the poorest tenants.

Readers who have watched inner-city neighborhoods decay over the past generation may find it hard to believe that poor tenants' housing really improved during this period. But confusing the fate of neighborhoods with the fate of individuals is a serious mistake. Boarded-up buildings and weed-filled lots show that fewer people want to live in a neighborhood, not that the people who used to live there now live in worse housing.

If we want to know how poor people's housing has changed, we must ignore buildings that have been torn down, burned, or abandoned and concentrate on those that are still inhabited. The buildings that have survived in America's worst neighborhoods are usually somewhat better than the ones that disappeared. The buildings to which people move when they leave these neighborhoods also tend to be more modern and better equipped than the buildings they left behind. The net result is that even poor tenants now live in somewhat better quarters.

Once we recognize that housing improved during the 1970s and 1980s, we have to ask how large a role these improvements played in pushing up rents. The most obvious way of answering this question is to look at the price index for rental housing prepared by the Bureau of Labor Statistics (BLS). This index, which measures annual rent increases in a large sample of units that have not undergone major renovations, rose 153 percent between 1973 and 1989. Tenants' median income, measured in current dollars, rose 156 percent during this period. Thus when tenants stayed in the same housing, their rents usually rose slightly less than their income.

The trouble with this approach is that most housing deteriorates over time. That is especially true if we exclude housing that has undergone major renovations. Not only does the typical building deteriorate, so do neighboring buildings. Tenants who stay in the same apartment for sixteen years are therefore likely to find not only that their own building is in worse shape than it was when they moved in but that the whole neighborhood has slipped. Tenants who want to avoid this gradual erosion in the quality of their environment usually have to keep moving to newer buildings in newer neighborhoods. When they do this, their rent rises faster than the BLS price index.[9]

Rather than relying on the BLS index, therefore, I have used the American Housing Survey to estimate rent changes in units with the same average characteristics as the units available in 1973. The physical and geographic characteristics measured in the AHS explain only half the variation in tenants' monthly rent, so my estimates probably miss some of the qualitative improvements that pushed up rents after 1973. The AHS figures should, however, set a lower bound on the likely value of these improvements.

Real rents in unsubsidized units rose 11 percent between 1973 and 1979 and another 20 percent between 1979 and 1989 (see Figure 4). Qualitative improvements account for about half this increase. Among low-income tenants in unsubsidized units, real rents rose even more, but that was because their housing improved more. Once we eliminate rent increases traceable to qualitative improvements, unsubsidized low-income tenants' real rent rose only 16 percent between 1973 and 1989. Most of this increase came during the 1970s. From 1979 to 1989 the increase was only 6 percent.

These estimates could overstate the true improvement in living conditions if, as many people believe, low-income tenants moved to better housing largely because their old neighborhoods were growing more dangerous. According to this theory, it cost more to buy any given level of safety in 1989 than in 1973. The AHS does not provide crime statistics for the neighborhoods in which low-income tenants lived. But we do know how crimes rates in general have changed since the early 1970s. These data do not suggest that the price of safety has risen.

Like the AHS, the Census Bureau's National Crime Victimization Survey (NCVS) began in 1973. Since then the NCVS has asked millions of Americans whether they were raped, robbed, or assaulted, and whether their house was burgled, during the past six months. The proportion reporting a rape, robbery, aggravated assault, or burglary did not change much between 1973 and 1981. After 1981, victimiza-

Figure 4. Percent Increases in Unsubsidized Rent, 1973–1989

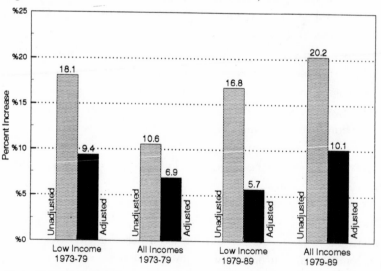

Source: Appendix Table A.3.

tion rates fell. The decline for household burglary and personal lar-
ceny (purse snatching, for example), was quite dramatic. There was
less decline for violent crimes, but the most serious forms of violence (rape and aggravated assault) did decline somewhat.[10] So did
murder.

The NCVS does not report victimization rates separately for low-
income tenants, but until the end of the 1980s victimization rates
declined for blacks as well as whites. The proportion of blacks who had
been victims of violence began to climb in 1990, but that obviously
cannot explain why tenants moved to better housing during the late
1970s or during the 1980s. Violence also climbed among people between the ages of twelve and twenty-four during the late 1980s. This
may have made parents more anxious to move, even though their own
chances of being raped, robbed, or murdered were falling.

The fact that burglary declined and that violence remained roughly
stable during the 1970s and 1980s will startle readers whose ideas about
crime come from either local police statistics or the summaries of those
statistics that the FBI releases every year. Although murder rates are no
higher today than in the mid-1970s, the police report many more rapes,
robberies, and aggravated assaults. This is partly because victims are
more likely to call the police and partly because the police have spent
billions of dollars computerizing their record keeping systems, so
crimes that get reported are more likely to become part of the official
record. Improved reporting and record-keeping plus highly selective
news reporting have, in turn, helped convince the public that their
neighborhoods are more dangerous.

It is also important to remember that while victimization has not
risen since 1974, murder rates suggest a big increase between 1964 and
1974. When violence increases, it may take years before people move
to a safer place. That seems particularly likely if, as many claim, moving
decisions are heavily influenced by individual experiences. If people
delay moving until they themselves have been mugged, many years have
to pass before increased violence exerts its full effect. But while this
argument suggests that moving could have been a delayed response to
much earlier increases in the crime rate, it does not suggest that people
who moved to safer neighborhoods during the 1970s and 1980s got
nothing in return. On the average, they ended up safer.

Why Did the Poor Pay More Rent?

In 1973 low-income tenants in unsubsidized housing already spent half their income on rent. Is it plausible that people who spent that much on rent would voluntarily move to even more expensive housing just to get more amenities or to escape risks they had lived with for years? Could these advantages possibly have been worth as much as the other things tenants gave up in order to move?

Many housing advocates think this a silly question. They assume poor tenants moved because they had no choice. Forced out of low-rent buildings by arson or abandonment, they could find no other equally cheap housing, and so they had to pay more. But if this image were accurate, the low-rent units that remained on the market should all have had long waiting lists and low vacancy rates. As we have seen, they did not. Vacancy rates in unsubsidized low-rent units were high throughout the 1970s and 1980s. In these circumstances I do not see how advocates can claim that low-income tenants had no choice.

An alternative explanation is that low-income tenants paid more because their overall resources were rising, even though their reported income was not. We can test this hypothesis using the Consumer Expenditure Survey (CES), which the Bureau of Labor Statistics conducted in 1972–73 and throughout the 1980s. The CES asks respondents for detailed information about their quarterly expenditures as well as their income.

Low-income tenants reported annual expenditure 50 to 75 percent higher than their annual income throughout the 1970s and 1980s. In 1988–1990, for example, tenants with household incomes below $10,000 reported monthly incomes averaging $503 and monthly expenditures averaging $909. The CES does not tell us how these tenants balanced their budgets, but most of them obviously had additional resources of some kind. That does not mean they were well off. Even $909 a month is hard living. But these tenants were not living on air, as their incomes might lead us to imagine.

The CES also shows that the disparity between these tenants' income and expenditure widened over time. In 1972–73, low-income tenants' expenditure exceeded their income by 53 percent. By 1988–1990 the difference was 74 percent. These disparities are partly traceable to the fact that some tenants fail to answer some of the income questions. But when we eliminate such tenants (which is possible only in the 1980s), the disparity between income and expenditure still increases over time. Among low-income tenants who answered all the income questions, expenditure exceeded income by 69 percent in 1988–1990 compared to only 47 percent in 1980–81.

Like the AHS, the Consumer Expenditure Survey shows that low-income tenants' rent rose faster than their reported income during the 1980s. But their rent did not rise any faster than their other expenditures. If anything, it rose slower. Rent and utilities accounted for 32 percent of total expenditure in 1972–73, 29 percent in 1980–81, and 28 percent in 1988–1990. Appendix Table A.4 displays these data in more detail.

I am not yet convinced that the increased rent burdens shown in Table 8 are spurious. But the CES does raises serious doubts about the view that rents have outstripped poor tenants' ability to pay. If the CES can be believed, there is no mystery about why poor tenants moved to better housing. They moved because they had more money to spend. The mystery is where that money came from. Perhaps these tenants had more unreported income. Perhaps they had more savings. We do not know.

Taking all the evidence together, I draw three conclusions. First, most cheap housing is also undesirable housing. Much of the increase in real rents over the past generation has been linked to improvements in the quality of housing. Those who calculate changes in rent burdens need to recognize that rising rents brought real benefits.

Second, those who claim that America experienced a growing shortage of low-rent housing during the 1970s and 1980s have not yet made a convincing case. Much cheap housing certainly disappeared, but that could have been because nobody wanted to live in it. Those who claim that cheap units were hard to find need to explain away the fact that landlords kept telling the Census Bureau that they had cheap units without tenants. Some claim that these units were not really available to tenants who wanted to rent them, but where is the evidence that this became more common?

Third, the apparent increase in rent burdens may be traceable to an increase in low-income tenants' unreported resources. The evidence for this hypothesis is not conclusive. The CES shows that poor tenants' total expenditures rose even faster than their rent, but no prudent person would draw strong conclusions from the CES alone.

Rent Burdens and Homelessness

In theory, any family that falls on hard times can become homeless. In practice, the problem is largely confined to single mothers. Single mothers are much poorer than married couples. Single mothers also tend to be poor in a different way. When a two-parent family is poor, it usually has a modest income and many children. That may mean eating a lot of beans and rice and putting several children in the same bed, but it seldom leads to homelessness. When single mothers are poor, they typically have fewer children and less income. That means they are more likely to become homeless.

After adjusting for inflation, the number of single mothers reporting cash incomes below either $2500 or $5000 rose dramatically during the 1980s (see Table 6). These women adopted all sorts of strategies to make ends meet. Many tried to cut their housing costs by getting a government subsidy, sharing space with a boyfriend, or doubling up with family members. Many also worked in the informal economy. Others got help from family members or from the father of their children. Some of these strategies cut their estimated rent burden. Others did not.

Table 9 uses the AHS to track rent burdens among single mothers who lived on their own, with no other adult in their household.[11] These mothers' real income lagged behind inflation from 1974 through 1985 but recovered somewhat in the late 1980s. Their real rent followed the opposite pattern, rising fairly steadily until 1987 and falling sharply in 1989. As a result, the typical mother's estimated rent burden climbed from 37 percent in 1974 to 60 percent in 1985 but then fell to 46 percent in 1989.

If rent burdens explained trends in family homelessness, Table 9 would lead to three predictions:

- Family homelessness should have increased during the late 1970s. That did not happen.
- Family homelessness should have increased even more dur-

Table 9. Monthly Income and Rent for Single Mothers Who Did Not Live with Another Adult, 1974–1989

Income and rent	1974	1975	1977	1979	1981	1983	1985	1987	1989
Median income	$833	$821	$806	$770	$707	$637	$616	$729	$744
Median rent	$309	$322	$335	$335	$337	$354	$371	$379	$342
Rent burden[a]	37%	39%	42%	44%	48%	56%	60%	52%	46%

Percent of single mothers reporting rent burdens above selected levels

	All mothers			Unsubsidized mothers			Unsubsidized mothers with income below $5000[b]		
Rent burden[a]	1974–79	1981–83	1985–89	1974–79	1981–83	1985–89	1974–79	1981–83	1985–89
Above 60%	16.1	26.6	28.1	17.8	28.9	29.8	75.5	87.8	88.6
Above 100%	7.3	13.7	15.2	8.2	14.0	15.0	49.9	61.8	61.1

Source: American Housing Survey. Samples include only unmarried female tenants with children under the age of eighteen whose household did not include another adult over the age of twenty-one.

a. Median rent as a percent of median income.

b. Income in 1989 dollars. Includes 16.3 percent of the sample in 1974–1979; 24.0 percent in 1981–1983; and 24.6 percent in 1985–1989.

ing the first half of the 1980s. That did happen, but the increase was quite small.

• Family homelessness should have declined after 1985. The opposite happened.

The weak connection between rent burdens and homelessness becomes even clearer when we compare 1981 to 1989. The typical single mother's rent burden fell from 48 percent in 1981 to 46 percent in 1989. Yet the number of homeless families rose from almost zero in 1981 to around 20,000 in 1989.

These figures describe what happened to the typical single mother. The bottom half of Table 9 shows the percentage of single mothers reporting rent burdens so high that homelessness appeared imminent in different periods. I show both the proportion spending more than 60 percent of their reported income on rent and the proportion spending more than 100 percent. Regardless of which criterion one chooses, the proportion of single mothers who seem on the verge of homelessness is higher during the 1980s than during the 1970s. But the proportion is only marginally higher in the late 1980s than in the early 1980s.

The single mothers most likely to show up in shelters are those with incomes below $5000. Roughly a quarter of all single mothers in households that contained no other adult told the AHS that their annual income was below $5000 in both the early and late 1980s. Table 9 shows that three-fifths of these families reported monthly rent and utility bills that exceeded their total monthly income for the previous year.[12]

Some of these households undoubtedly have other income that they do not report to the Census Bureau. If a single mother has a live-in boyfriend whose presence she does not advertise, her household income—and her ability to pay rent—will be higher than what she reports to the AHS. Likewise, if she is collecting welfare while getting money under the table from her parents, the father of her children, or off-the-books employment, her monthly rent may well exceed her reported income.[13]

But deliberate deception cannot be the whole story, because many single mothers in subsidized housing also report very high rent burdens. Current law limits rent to 30 percent of the tenant's income in most federally subsidized housing.[14] Although some families undoubtedly conceal part of their income from the local housing authority in order to keep their rent down, they have no incentive to conceal income from the Census Bureau once they report it to the local authorities. In most cases, therefore, rents in subsidized units should be no more than 30 percent of what the tenant reports to the AHS. Yet a sixth of all single mothers in subsidized housing reported that their gross rent was more than 100 percent of their income in 1985–1989, and another tenth reported gross rents between 60 and 100 percent of their income. Such findings suggest that haste, indifference, and clerical errors play as large a role as deliberate deception in exaggerating tenants' rent burdens.[15]

The Consumer Expenditure Survey again provides a useful check on the AHS. Among single mothers interviewed during the 1980s who answered every income question, 14 percent said their gross rent was more than half their income, but only 2.2 percent said it was more than half their total expenditure. Among those reporting incomes below $5000, 54 percent said their rent was more than half their income, but only 2.5 percent said it was more than half their total expenditure.[16]

Although the CES suggests that the AHS overstates single mothers' rent burden, the two surveys still tell broadly consistent stories about trends during the 1980s. Both show that single mothers' rent rose faster than their income in the first half of the decade and slower in the second half. The proportion of single mothers whose rent exceeded half their total expenditures rose from 1.2 percent in 1980–81 to 3.6 percent in 1984–85 and then fell to 1.4 percent in 1988–1990. Thus if rent burdens were a crucial factor in family homelessness, we would expect the number of families in shelters to have peaked around 1985. That is clearly not what happened.

Nonetheless, everyone believes that rent increases played a major role in the spread of family homelessness. If this belief is false, its persistence requires an explanation. The simplest explanation is that what I have been calling "real" incomes and rents are not real at all. These terms describe statistical fictions, created by adjusting current income or rent to take account of the estimated rate of inflation in the economy as a whole. No ordinary citizen knows the rate of inflation in the economy as a whole. As a result, no one knows—or much cares—how their real income or real rent has changed over time. When a single mother finds that her rent has risen 7 percent while her welfare check has risen 2 percent, she does not ask whether her real income has risen or fallen. She just knows that her rent has risen faster than her income. She therefore blames her economic plight on rising rents. Most other people do the same thing.

While real incomes and rents have no meaning on the streets, they do help us see some things that we could not otherwise see. In particular, they help us see that the main problem facing single mothers during the 1980s was legislative stinginess rather than landlords' greed. Among single mothers with incomes below $10,000 who lived in unsubsidized housing, real rents rose 13 percent during the 1980s (see Appendix Table A.3), and half this increase was attributable to qualitative improvements. That makes it hard to blame the increase in family homelessness on changes in the housing market. I therefore believe that the main source of single mothers' housing problems during the 1980s was state legislators' growing reluctance to subsidize families in which the parents did not live together.

9. Budget Cuts and Rent Control

Like every puzzling social problem, homelessness evokes strong instinctive responses from both liberals and conservatives. Liberals see it as evidence that the government has not done enough to provide affordable housing. Many go further and pin the blame on the Reagan Administration, which they think gutted the government's low-income housing programs. Conservatives, in contrast, see homelessness as evidence that the government has done too much. Some blame homelessness on a pervasive culture of dependency, created by an excessively generous welfare state. Others blame building codes and local rent-control ordinances that they think discourage entrepreneurs from housing the poor. Still others blame the shelter system itself.

What Happened to Federal Housing Programs?

Despite the fact that vacancy rates in low-rent private housing have been quite stable, the shortage of such housing remains a staple of liberal writing about housing and homelessness. Two Washington-based advocacy groups, the Center for Budget and Policy Priorities (CBPP) and the Low Income Housing Information Service (LIHIS), have been particularly influential advocates of this view. Their position is summarized in *A Place to Call Home: The Low Income Housing Crisis Continues,* written in 1991 by Edward Lazere, Paul Leonard, Cushing Dolbeare, and Barry Zigas.

Table 10. Number of Tenants with Low Income, Low Rent, and Government
Subsidies, 1973, 1979, and 1989 (Numbers in millions)

Tenants and units	1973	1979	1989
All tenants	24.7	28.4	33.8
Tenants with annual income between $1 and $9,999[a]	6.3	8.0	9.1
Tenants in subsidized housing[b]	2.0	2.9	4.2
Occupied units costing less than $250 a month[a]	7.8	7.4	7.7
Percent of tenants with income below $10,000 paying less than $250 a month	58.1%	49.3%	47.4%

Source: See Table 8.
  a. 1989 dollars.
  b. Public housing or rent subsidy.

Lazere and his colleagues contrast the number of low-income tenants (family income below $10,000) with the number of low-rent housing units (rent below $250 a month). As Table 10 indicates, the number of low-rent housing units was essentially stable from 1973 to 1989, while the number of low-income tenants rose sharply.[1] Lazere and his colleagues argue that this change made it much harder for low-income tenants to find housing they could afford.

The last row of Table 10 shows that while the fraction of low-income tenants living in low-rent housing fell from 1973 to 1979, it did not fall much during the 1980s. This stability reflects the fact that low-rent housing was redistributed during the 1980s, with a larger share going to low-income tenants and a smaller share going to more affluent tenants. This redistribution was a byproduct of federal intervention in the housing market.

The supply of cheap privately owned rental units contracted during the 1970s and 1980s. But as Table 10 shows, the supply of government-subsidized housing grew. In addition, subsidized housing was increasingly allocated to the very poor. As a result, 32 percent of all low-income tenants were getting some kind of government subsidy in 1989, compared to only 21 percent in 1979 and 14 percent in 1973 (see Table 8). Rent in most federally subsidized housing was limited by law to 30 percent of family income during the 1980s, so most low-income tenants paid less than $250 a month.[2]

Yet despite the growth of federal programs during these years, *A Place to Call Home* starts its discussion of Washington's role in the low-income housing crisis by claiming that "federal housing programs were cut sharply in the 1980s." The authors support this claim by noting that "appropriations for HUD's subsidized housing programs fell from a peak of $32.2 billion in fiscal year 1978 to $11.7 billion in fiscal year 1991."[3] This assertion is correct. But unless you are a housing junkie, it is also misleading. Contrary to what a lay reader might imagine, "appropriations" are not a measure of how much HUD spends in a given year on housing subsidies. Instead, appropriations measure the increase in HUD's future commitments. A cut in appropriations is not, therefore, a cut in the size of HUD's programs; it is a cut in the rate at which these programs will grow during the years ahead.

When HUD subsidizes either a housing unit or a family, it makes a long-term commitment. The estimated long-term cost of the new commitments that Congress authorizes is HUD's "net budget authority," commonly known as its appropriation. When this money is actually spent, it is known as an outlay. Appropriations are thus a set of promises; outlays redeem those promises.

HUD made a lot of promises while Gerald Ford and Jimmy Carter were in the White House. Between 1977 and 1981 HUD authorized 2.0 million new units of subsidized housing for low-income tenants.[4] Because both HUD and most local housing agencies move very slowly, many of these units only became available to tenants after President Carter left office. The number of low-income tenants getting federal subsidies would therefore have continued to rise during Reagan's first term even if Congress had never authorized another penny of new federal spending.

If the Reagan Administration had had its way, new appropriations for low-income housing programs would have stopped after 1981. In reality, though, Congress kept making new commitments throughout the Reagan and Bush years. From 1982 through 1989 Congress authorized another 1.0 million units of subsidized low-income housing. That was less than when Carter was in the White House, but it was still growth, not shrinkage. Furthermore, when the commitments that HUD had made during the 1970s began to run out in 1989, Congress renewed them all.

Figure 5 traces the budgetary consequences of all this. Net budget authority fell dramatically, just as Lazere and his colleagues indicate. But actual outlays for low-income housing, measured in constant dollars, rose from $9 billion in 1980 to $18 billion in 1992, and the number of federally subsidized rental units grew from 2.9 to 4.7 million—points that Lazere and his colleagues mention only in passing.[5] Using the growth measure that CBPP and LIHIS favor, which is the number of new tenants assisted, federal programs for low-income tenants grew more than 60 percent between 1980 and 1992. That was far less than the increase during the 1970s, but it was still growth, not shrinkage.

The slow but steady growth of low-income housing subsidies under Presidents Reagan and Bush was one of the few liberal success stories in a generally conservative era. Federal outlays for low-income housing rose faster than outlays for either social security or defense.[6] Yet the congressional Democrats responsible for this growth never tried to claim credit for it. They seem to have concluded that the best way to keep housing subsidies growing was to claim they were shrinking.

Figure 5. Changes in HUD Expenditures, 1977–1992

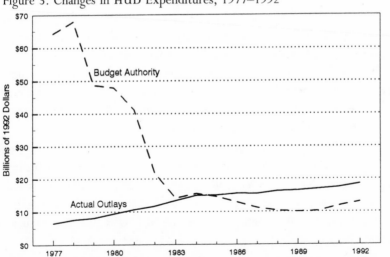

Source: House Committee on Ways and Means, *1992 Green Book,* pp. 1680–81. Net budget authority for 1989–1992 excludes renewals of expiring Section 8 contracts. Outlays for 1985 exclude a $14 billion charge to pay off capital costs for the construction and modernization of public housing incurred between 1974 and 1985.

Like Lazere and his colleagues, Democratic legislators emphasized the decline in HUD's net budget authority, not the increase in its actual outlays.

Blaming Reagan for cutting low-income housing programs had all kinds of political advantages. To begin with, it allowed the Democrats to blame the Republicans for increased homelessness. Had the Democrats tried to claim credit for expanding the government's low-income housing programs, the tables would have been turned, and the Republicans would have been able to cite homelessness as evidence that federal housing programs were counter-productive. In this debate both sides seemed to agree on at least one principle: simple distortions are more politically persuasive than complicated truths. That principle may be correct. But if it is, the odds are heavily against our doing anything effective either to help the homeless or to solve most other social problems.

Partisan Liberalism Run Amok

Partisan considerations have shaped the discussion of housing and homelessness at the local level as well. In 1991, for example, the Mayor of New York, David Dinkins, appointed a commission on homelessness chaired by Andrew Cuomo, who is now an Assistant Secretary of Housing and Urban Development in the Clinton Administration. The Commission's report made a number of sensible suggestions about how New York City should revamp its shelter system. But when the Commission sought to explain why New York had so little cheap housing, it settled for bashing the Republicans.

The most important reason New York lacked cheap housing, according to the Commission, was that "the federal government, historically the provider of low cost housing, has abandoned the business."[7] The Commission backed up this claim with data on declines in HUD's net budget authority—data provided by the Low Income Housing Information Service.

Even if we set aside the canard about cutbacks in low-income housing programs, the claim that the federal government was historically the main provider of low-cost housing is breathtakingly wrong. Private landlords have built and operated most of New York's cheap housing ever since the Dutch bought out the Indians. What changed during the 1970s and 1980s, as anyone could see driving through the South Bronx or Brooklyn, was not that the federal government abandoned the low-cost housing business but that private landlords did so. The city took over thousands of buildings that private landlords no longer thought worth maintaining, and landlords torched many more for insurance money. Anyone who wants to explain why cheap housing is so much scarcer in New York than elsewhere in the country needs to explain abandonment. The Cuomo Commission simply ignored it.

The Commission's discussion of New York's housing shortage is not crucial to its recommendations and appears near the end of its report. Nonetheless, the repetition of liberal fairy tales in a report signed by eminent businessmen does raise intriguing questions. Did the members of the Commission read the report? Did they believe what it said? Did they ask anyone in their employ to check it for accuracy? If they did not, was this because they did not think accuracy mattered? I assume Mayor Dinkins appointed eminent businessmen to the Commission in order to persuade the rest of the business community that the Commission was not in the hands of wild-eyed liberals. But if members of blue-ribbon commissions do not verify the contents of the reports they sign, why should their signatures reassure anyone?

Rent Control

In *The Excluded Americans* William Tucker provides a more conservative view of New York City's housing problems.[8] As Tucker notes, New York (which he calls Moscow-on-the-Hudson) has always had an unusually high proportion of middle-class tenants. That means New York tenants have more political influence than tenants in other big cities. When the federal government ended rent control after World War II, every other major American city eventually let it lapse. New York kept it. Because New York's affluent tenants had so much political influence, the city also administered rent control (and later "rent stabilization") in such a way as to protect their interests.

Every year the city allowed landlords in regulated buildings to raise rents by a fixed percentage, which was usually less than the average increase in the open market. This pattern created a widening disparity between regulated and unregulated rents, but the magnitude of this disparity varied by neighborhood. In gentrifying neighborhoods where market rents were rising faster than the citywide average, tenants in regulated buildings reaped big windfalls. In deteriorating neighborhoods where market rents were rising less than the citywide average, Tucker reports, living in a regulated building made far less difference.

If rent control had merely redistributed money from landlords to affluent tenants, as Tucker's analysis implies, it would have left the poor almost untouched. But rent control may well have hurt the poor in other important ways. Because long-time residents of a neighborhood have more political influence than newcomers, New York legislators were more concerned with protecting sitting tenants than with protecting new arrivals. The law therefore put tight limits on rent increases for old tenants while allowing larger increases when a new tenant moved in. Unfortunately, that gave landlords a financial incentive to drive out sitting tenants. To prevent such abuses, legislators had to make evictions almost impossible.

Rules that make evictions difficult usually protect all tenants, good and bad. Protecting bad tenants hurts not only landlords but good tenants. Because New York City took forever to evict tenants who failed to pay their rent, landlords' revenue fell. That forced many landlords to cut services. Because they could not evict tenants who sold drugs, robbed their neighbors, or treated their building as an oversized dumpster, many landlords gave up trying to run a "respectable" building and settled for running a dump. Thus while rent control did little to lower poor tenants' rents, it may well have reduced the number of cheap apartments in which the landlord tried to keep the building safe and presentable.

Tucker also stresses one other effect of rent control that most analysts ignore, which is the way it poisons relations between landlords and tenants. In a normal housing market, tenants who do not like their landlord simply move. But when rent control keeps a city's rents artificially low, demand for housing soon exceeds the supply, and vacancy rates fall almost to zero. Meanwhile, many landlords cut back maintenance and services, making tenants unhappy. But these unhappy tenants cannot simply move, because there are no vacant units nearby, or none at prices comparable to what they are now paying. No matter how unhappy they are, therefore, tenants stay and fight. Since landlords cannot evict aggrieved tenants, they fight back. In due course landlord-tenant warfare occupies a large portion of everyone's time and energy.

Although Tucker's indictment of rent control is persuasive, he pushes his critique much too far when he tries to show that rent control contributes to homelessness. Using the 1984 HUD survey that asked local informants to guess how many people in their city were homeless, he shows that informants reported higher levels of homelessness in cities with rent control than in cities without it. But it does not follow that rent control causes homelessness.

To begin with, cities with rent control almost all have a more liberal political climate than cities without it. Since liberals consistently claim that the national rate of homelessness is high while conservatives consistently claim that it is much lower, one would expect to find the same pattern at the local level. Thus even if cities dominated by liberals and conservatives had exactly the same rates of homelessness, one would expect to get higher estimates in cities dominated by liberals. The correlation between rent control and homelessness may therefore be spurious.

Even if rent control really is correlated with homelessness, it does not follow that one causes the other. The historical record certainly raises doubts about such a link. New York City has had the most stringent rent control in the country since the late 1940s, yet homelessness did not become a major problem there until the late 1970s. No other major city reinstituted rent control until the 1970s, when inflation began pushing up rents. If rent control takes thirty years to drive up homelessness, as the New York experience suggests, it should not yet have had any effect outside New York.

Nor does statistical analysis support Tucker's causal argument. John Quigley has shown that the correlation between rent control and homelessness is explained by two facts.[9] First, cities with rent control have lower vacancy rates than cities without it, and low vacancy rates are associated with homelessness. Second, cities with rent control have higher rents than cities without it, and high rents are also associated with homelessness.

The correlations involving vacancy rates are consistent with Tucker's argument. If rent control reduces rents below their market level, as it is supposed to do, vacancy rates should fall. New York's experience illustrates this principle. It has a strong rent-control law and almost no vacant housing. It is also easy to see why low vacancy rates would cause homelessness. When landlords have long waiting lists and cannot raise rents, they become much choosier about the tenants they will accept. Many refuse to take anyone on welfare. Others will take welfare mothers who have a record of paying on time but not those who have recently been evicted.

The correlations involving rent levels are harder to reconcile with Tucker's argument. If rent control lowers vacancy rates by lowering rents, it cannot also push rents higher than they otherwise would be. If rent control is correlated with high rents, as Tucker's data suggest, the most likely explanation is not that rent control pushes up rents but that rapidly rising rents lead to rent control. Since most cities that adopt rent control pursue policies that lower rents only a little, one would expect cities with rent control to have above-average rents.

If rent control lowers both rents and vacancy rates, as seems likely, its net effect on homelessness is uncertain. Conservatives who want to blame homelessness on the government should look elsewhere, concentrating on regulations that restrict the kind of housing landlords can provide rather than regulations that restrict the price at which it is offered.

10. Do Shelters Cause Homelessness?

As far as I can tell, the spread of homelessness among single adults was a byproduct of five related changes: the elimination of involuntary commitment, the eviction of mental hospital patients who had nowhere to go, the advent of crack, increases in long-term joblessness, and political restrictions on the creation of flophouses. Among families, three factors appear to have been important: the spread of single motherhood, the erosion of welfare recipients' purchasing power, and perhaps crack.

Taken together, these changes seem to me adequate to explain what happened during the early 1980s, but they do not quite explain what happened later in the decade. When the economy began to recover, homelessness should have declined. Crack was the only major new factor in the equation after 1984. While crack certainly made some people homeless, it cannot explain most of the increase, especially among single mothers. We must therefore consider another possibility. Perhaps improvements in the shelter system have encouraged homelessness.[1]

By the late 1980s America had created a network of shelters and soup kitchens that serviced between 200,000 and 300,000 people a day. These institutions tried to improve the lives of the homeless, and they apparently succeeded. When the cost of something falls, demand usually rises. That truism holds regardless of whether the costs are monetary, emotional, or physical. When the expected cost of crime or adultery falls, more people engage in them. When homelessness becomes less painful, people are less willing to sacrifice their pride, their self-respect, or their cocaine fix to avoid it.

Those who see the homeless as passive victims of circumstances beyond their control often react to this argument with a mixture of fury and disbelief. To say that people choose to become homeless seems indecent. But the homeless are not just passive victims. They make choices, like everyone else. The choices open to the homeless are far worse than those open to most Americans, but they are still choices.

Consider homeless families. About two million single-parent families currently live in someone else's home.[2] In a sense, all these families are already homeless. Most are desperate to find a place of their own. To do this they must either increase their income or get into subsidized housing. The number of families with incomes low enough to qualify for a subsidy is far larger than the number of subsidized units actually available, so there is always a waiting list. Doubled-up families will use every strategy imaginable to reach the head of this list.

Federal law gives priority to certain kinds of applicants, including the homeless. In many communities the homeless get very high priority. If doubled-up families know this, some of them will begin wondering how long they would have to spend in a shelter to get a permanent subsidy. If their present situation is bad enough and the wait for subsidized housing seems likely to be substantially shorter in a shelter, some will make the move.

Those who think this sounds fanciful should ponder the experience of New York. During the 1980s, the Koch Administration housed most of the city's homeless families in welfare hotels, forcing them to wait well over a year for permanent housing. These hotels were nasty, dangerous places, so only women in extraordinarily difficult situations moved into them, and many moved out within a few weeks. The minority who stayed got the handful of subsidized units the city had allocated to the homeless. This rationing system caused a great deal of misery, but it did ensure that the few available subsidized units went to the most desperate families. Unfortunately, that was not the way the courts or the press saw the system. To them, the long wait was not a rationing system but evidence of bureaucratic callousness, incompetence, or both.

By the time Mayor Koch left office in 1989, the city was under

court order to move the homeless out of welfare hotels, and the Bush
Administration was trying to cut off federal funds for such places. Soon
after David Dinkins became Mayor, the city began reducing the wait for
permanent housing. At first this policy lowered the number of families
in welfare hotels. But as the waiting period for permanent housing
shortened, more families began entering the system. Some actually told
inquiring journalists that they had moved into a shelter or a welfare
hotel in order to qualify for subsidized housing. Since the supply of
subsidized units was limited, the waiting period grew longer and the
number of families in welfare hotels climbed again.[3]

Even when homelessness is not a route to better housing, creating
family shelters will pull some single mothers out of conventional
housing. Shelters for battered women are the most obvious example.
The whole point of these shelters is to lure women out of conventional
housing and into a shelter. If this effort succeeds, the number of people
counted as homeless will rise. The women in question are better off,
and so is society. But that is not always obvious to casual observers, who
find it easier to ignore these women's plight when they suffer behind
locked doors. Once they are officially homeless, their troubles become,
at least in some small measure, our troubles.

Physical abuse is not the only force pushing families into shelters
and welfare hotels. Single mothers who have been staying with relatives
or friends may want to leave because someone in their host's household
is molesting their daughter, because the building has become so dangerous they do not want their children there, or because they can see that
their presence is wrecking their host's family life. If shelters become
available, some of these women will leave. The better the shelter system
gets, the more women will use it.

America's efforts to improve living conditions among the homeless
may even have pulled more single adults into the system. This is not
because we have offered homeless single adults subsidized housing.
Except for the mentally ill and the elderly, single adults still have almost
no access to federally subsidized housing. But even the prospect of a
free bed may be enough to pull some single adults out of other people's
homes.

The creation of shelters and soup kitchens is especially likely to
make a difference when men are doubled up with reluctant hosts who

want them to leave. Proud men find such situations almost unendurable. If a community gives them an alternative, some will use it. Free local shelters may also make reluctant hosts more willing to throw out unwanted guests, especially if they cause trouble. Better shelters and easier access to soup kitchens may also have reduced the chances that the homeless will return to households where they are not welcome.

This argument should not be misunderstood. I am not suggesting that anyone prefers living in a shelter to living in a place of their own. But for the poorest of the poor these are seldom the choices. For them, the choice is usually between different kinds of homelessness: living in someone else's home, living in a shelter, or living on the streets. Each of these alternatives has different costs. If we make one of these options less costly than it was before, more people will choose it.

Improving the lot of the homeless may even change the behavior of some people who have been living on their own. Nobody, rich or poor, wants to spend all their money on housing if they can avoid it. If shelters become more attractive or more widely available, or if changes in police practice make the streets more hospitable, some people who have been living in very cheap hotels may well pass fewer nights in hotels and more nights in places that are free.

Homelessness also feeds on itself. For those of us who have never been homeless, the prospect is fearsome. We do not know our way around the shelters, soup kitchens, and other places where the homeless congregate. People who have already been homeless are probably more confident that they will be able to cope if they become homeless again. A man who is staying with his sister and constantly biting his tongue when she complains about his behavior may exercise less self-control once he has spent some time on the streets, because his need for self-respect now outweighs his fear of being evicted.

By 1990, 5.3 percent of all grownups said they had slept in a shelter or on the streets at some point in their adult life.[4] The age distribution of these individuals suggests that far fewer adults had such experiences fifteen years ago. The more people learn about coping with homelessness, the easier the boundary is to cross.

11. Some Partial Solutions

Although I doubt that changes in the housing market played a major role in the spread of homelessness, better housing is still the first step in dealing with the problem. Regardless of why people are on the streets, giving them a place to live that offers a modicum of privacy and stability is usually the most important thing we can do to improve their lives. Without stable housing, nothing else is likely to work. If people have housing, the rest of their life may improve. Even if it does not, at least they have a home.

Unlike programs that seek to improve people's character, programs that seek to improve their housing are comparatively easy to devise and evaluate. The simplest test is whether people use them. Burt's surveys suggest that only a third of homeless single adults slept in shelters on an average night in 1987. The proportion may now be more like half, but even that is hardly a resounding endorsement of the shelter system.[1]

Making Shelters Habitable

If housing is as important to the homeless as I claim, their reluctance to use shelters requires explanation. Some advocates still believe the problem is mainly a lack of beds, but HUD's shelter surveys do not suggest that this is a pervasive problem. In September 1988, shelter managers told HUD that 35 percent of their beds had been vacant over the course of the previous year. Even in January 1984, when the weather was cold and the number of shelter beds was far lower than in 1987–88,

managers reported that 30 percent of their beds were empty.[2] Not all
shelters have vacancies. Shelters are free, so the best ones fill up first.
Empty beds are concentrated in the worst big-city shelters and in
smaller communities where demand is unpredictable.

Still, bed shortages cannot explain the pattern of shelter use.
HUD's 1988 survey found that the typical family shelter was full two
nights out of three, while the typical shelter for single men was full only
one night out of three.[3] Yet homeless families almost always spent the
night in shelters during 1988, whereas homeless men mostly spent the
night elsewhere. Nor can bed shortages explain why so many single men
never use shelters at all. Of the 445 homeless adults Burt interviewed
in congregating sites, 292 had not used a shelter at any time during the
previous week. How are we to explain this?

While most shelters for single adults have empty beds most of the
time, they seldom admit everyone who comes to the door. As far as I
know, New York, Philadelphia, and Washington are the only major cities
that have tried to guarantee everyone shelter. Both Philadelphia and
Washington have now abandoned this policy. Most shelters are run by
private groups that set their own rules and turn away people who cannot
or will not conform to these rules.[4] Many exclude people who appear
to be drunk, hallucinating, or high on drugs. Many bar people who have
given them grief in the past. These policies keep out a significant fraction
of the homeless on any given night. And once a shelter has turned a
man away or asked him to leave, he is often reluctant to come back,
even when he is sane enough or sober enough to be admitted. The
cumulative effect of such policies is substantial.

But it does not follow that the proportion of the homeless sleeping
in shelters would rise if they adopted less restrictive admissions policies.
Quite the contrary. Shelters are like neighborhoods: once "undesirables"
move in, everyone else tries to move out. No sensible person wants to
spend the night in a dormitory that admits all comers, drunk or sober,
sane or mad, violent or catatonic. One has only to look at New York
City to see where such a policy leads.

When people must live in a crowded space that offers no privacy,
they need all kinds of written or unwritten rules to ensure that sleep
is possible, that quarrels do not escalate, and that the strong do not
victimize the weak. A shelter that does not have such rules or cannot

enforce them soon turns into a Hobbesian nightmare. Not even the homeless want to sleep in such places. Yet a large proportion of the homeless also avoid shelters with strict rules. Many find such rules patronizing, difficult to follow, or both. Everyone wants the stranger in the next bed to be unarmed and sober. But no one wants to be frisked or have their breath smelled to determine whether they themselves are unarmed and sober. There is no easy way out of this dilemma. A congregate shelter that admits everyone will scare away many of its potential clients. A congregate shelter that makes strict rules will also drive away many of its potential clients. The only solution is to move beyond congregate shelters, giving everyone a private space of their own, the way the old cubicle hotels did.

To do this we must spend more money. But taxpayers will only agree to spend more money if we ask more of the homeless in return. That seems to me perfectly reasonable. Simply warehousing the homeless in better places would improve their material lives a bit, but it would do nothing to restore their self-respect or reintegrate them into the larger society. For that, they must be given responsibilities of some kind. This means devising different policies for different groups, depending on what we can reasonably expect them to do in return for better housing. At the outset, we need to distinguish between families with children, single adults whom we can expect to work, and single adults whom we do not expect to work.

Families with Children

The housing problems of families with children are inseparable from the larger problem of welfare reform. The simplest way to eliminate homelessness among these families would be to raise real cash welfare benefits to the levels that prevailed in the mid-1970s, so recipients could afford private housing. But that is not going to happen. While three quarters of all Americans say they oppose further cuts in welfare benefits, three quarters also oppose raising benefits.[5]

Over the past quarter century, a growing majority of Americans has come to believe that we should make single mothers find jobs. A 1993 survey conducted for the Associated Press found that 84 percent of American adults favored a work requirement for welfare recipients, including those with preschool children. A Yankelovich survey found equally large majorities favoring a work requirement, with almost no variation by race, income, or political party.[6] This idea is not new. Congress made its first effort to get recipients "off the welfare rolls and onto payrolls" in 1967, and it has been trying to do the same thing ever since.

If we want to solve single mothers' economic problems by making them take jobs, we must first disabuse ourselves of two mistaken beliefs. First, we must stop imagining that putting single mothers to work will make the country richer or generate extra money to pay these mothers' bills. Single mothers now care for their children. If we make them take jobs, someone else will have to care for their children while they are at work. We will have to pay the people who watch these children more than we now pay their mothers to do the same job. That is going to cost the taxpayer more money.

Working mothers who left their children in a nonrelative's home paid an average of $64 a week in 1990. Those who used childcare centers paid $76 a week.[7] Meanwhile, cash welfare benefits for a mother with two children averaged $42 per child per week.[8] In most states, therefore, paying single mothers to care for their own children was a bargain. That is one reason why states have been so reluctant to implement federal legislation aimed at putting more welfare mothers to work. In order to make every mother with preschool children work, states would usually have to spend more for childcare than they would save on welfare payments. While some surveys suggest that voters favor this approach, state legislators have refused to pursue it.[9]

Those who want to solve welfare mothers' economic problems by putting them to work must also think more realistically about the cost of raising a family. The fact that cash welfare benefits are typically $300 to $400 a month for a mother with two children seems to have convinced a lot of people that families can really live on such sums. That delusion leads to an equally illusory corollary: if single mothers can live on welfare, they can also live on what they would earn in a minimum-wage job. Both assumptions are wrong.

Over the past few years Kathryn Edin and Laura Lein have interviewed hundreds of single mothers in Cambridge, Charleston, Chicago, and San Antonio. Unlike the Census Bureau, they interviewed people who had reason to trust them. As a result, mothers provided budgets in which their income matched their expenditures. Edin and Lane find that urban welfare mothers typically need about twice as much cash as they get from welfare. Mothers get this extra money from off-the-books employment, family members, boyfriends, and absent fathers. In 1989– 1992, mothers with two or more children spent an average of $11,000 a year. Outside San Antonio, hardly anyone got by on less than $10,000. Budgets were much lower in San Antonio, but material hardship—including hunger—was also more common.[10]

When single mothers worked, they needed even more income because they now had to pay for transportation to work, appropriate workplace clothing, childcare, and medical care. (Their jobs rarely provided medical insurance, and even those that did usually expected workers to pay a large part of the cost.) Taxes and social security aside, working mothers with two or more children typically spent $15,000 a year. Hardly any got by on less than $12,000. Work yielded only two significant material advantages: working mothers had better wardrobes, and they were more likely to own cars. Working mothers also spent more time with adults and less time with their children, but while some thought of this as a benefit, others saw it as a cost.

If we allow for taxes and social security, welfare mothers almost all need a steady job paying at least $7 an hour to make ends meet from work alone. Most would have to earn $8 or $9. Today's homeless mothers are never going to get jobs like that in the private sector. The only way they could earn such wages would be for society to create such jobs in the public or the nonprofit sector and reserve them for needy mothers. That seems to me politically inconceivable in a society with as little sense of social solidarity and as much commitment to competitive labor markets as ours.

Unskilled single mothers currently earn about $5 an hour. Job training raises a mother's chances of finding a job, but it seldom has much effect on her hourly wages.[11] Even if an unskilled single mother works full time, her annual earnings are unlikely to exceed $10,000. If the economy is in trouble, as it often is, she may earn even less.

If we want unskilled single mothers to take paid jobs instead of caring for their children, we will have to make up the difference between what they can earn and what they need to make ends meet.

There are many different ways of doing this. The Earned Income Tax Credit, which the Clinton Administration has just expanded, is one good approach. But we also need to provide noncash benefits of various kinds: food stamps, housing subsidies, medical insurance, and childcare. Overall, we will have to spend substantially more than we are spending now, because we will not only have to subsidize mothers who currently get welfare but also those who are already working.

Since some single mothers already work at low-wage jobs without government help, skeptics may wonder why today's welfare mothers would need such help if they worked. The answer is that the unskilled single mothers who currently support themselves without government help almost all get help elsewhere: free childcare from a relative, regular child support from an absent father, or free housing from their parents, for example. Others have unusually low expenses because they can walk to work, because their family is unusually healthy, or because alcohol, caffeine, and nicotine do not attract them. If every working mother had all these advantages, all could get by without public assistance. But for those who are not that lucky, some form of government help is crucial.

America may eventually create a system in which every single mother can support her family from a combination of minimum-wage work and government benefits. But doing this will take at least a decade and probably longer. Meanwhile, we need to help families that cannot keep a roof over their heads. The most direct approach is to expand HUD's rent-subsidy programs so that they reach all families with incomes below half the local median. No one knows exactly what this would cost, because no one knows how many of those who report low incomes to the Census Bureau would provide similar financial information to a local housing authority. Nor do we know how many of those who are legally eligible would actually apply. My rough guess is that covering everyone with an income below half the local median would double HUD's current $18 billion budget for low-income housing.

Congress is unlikely to increase HUD's budget by anything like $18 billion in the next few years. But HUD could also help more families by spending its current budget more equitably. HUD currently requires subsidized tenants to spend 30 percent of their income on housing. For those in private housing, HUD normally makes up the difference between this required contribution and the actual rent, so long as the rent is below what it calls the "fair market rent" for the area. HUD sets its fair market rents close to the local median, so if tenants get any assistance they often get quite a lot. As a result, HUD's $18 billion is not sufficient to help everyone who is in principle eligible. One easy way to help more families would be for HUD to put a lower ceiling on the amount of money it will give any one family.

Such a ceiling could conflict with another important goal of federal housing policy, which is—or at least should be—to reduce racial and economic segregation. If fair market rents are set too low, nobody who gets a HUD subsidy will be able to live in a good neighborhood. A sensible compromise might be to retain higher ceilings in middle-income neighborhoods while setting lower ceilings in poorer neighborhoods. That would provide extra help to poor families who want to buy their children better schooling or safer streets but not to those who want an extra bedroom or a nicer building in a bad neighborhood.

Childless Adults

When we turn from families to single adults, we need to begin by asking who can do useful work and who cannot. In principle, almost everyone can do something useful, and most people of working age (including the disabled) are better off when they have a job. But creating jobs for people who now get disability benefits would usually cost more than simply giving them cash. Since that seems unlikely in today's fiscal climate, I concentrate on halfway measures.

Even if we set aside those who are (or should be) eligible for disability benefits under current law, most of the homeless have characteristics that make them the last hired and first fired. That means they cannot expect to find steady work unless the labor market is very tight—a condition that has been quite unusual in the United States over the past hundred years. Except at the peak of the business cycle, most such people must scramble to find even casual jobs at low wages. Often they cannot get any work at all.

Better education and job training could make some of these workers more attractive to employers. But employers judge job applicants in competitive terms. If today's homeless acquire characteristics that make them look like better risks, other workers will slip to the end of the queue. In a competitive labor market, someone always has to be the last hired and first fired. Training schemes can rearrange the queue, but they cannot eliminate it. That means we must try to make life at the end of the queue more endurable rather than just helping people change places.

The problems of most jobless adults are intimately bound up with what economists call labor-market flexibility. A flexible labor market is one in which labor unions are weak, employers can hire and fire at will, and new workers are easy to find. For economists, this kind of flexibility is a good thing, because it encourages efficient use of labor power, which they seem to regard as an infinitely divisible and rearrangeable good, like electric power. Flexibility of this kind is widely cited as the reason why America created so many new jobs during the 1980s, while Europe created very few despite a comparable increase in economic output. European firms found it cheaper to raise the productivity, wages, and benefits of the workers already on their payrolls. As a result, wages and unemployment climbed together.

Labor-market flexibility also has a dark side: it guarantees that some workers will never find steady employment. In the nineteenth century Marx christened this group the lumpen proletariat. Until relatively recently, American sociologists called them the lower class. Today many Americans refer to them as the "underclass." Regardless of how we label them, their troubles play a central role in homelessness. Because they cannot find steady jobs, they cannot afford to internalize the work ethic or link their self-respect to their job performance. Many leave the labor market entirely. Others treat work as no more than a way of picking up a few dollars as needed. The side effects of this adaptation include depression, rage, alcoholism, drug addiction, and domestic violence.

Because America's labor market has traditionally been more flexible than Europe's, we have traditionally had a larger underclass. After World War II, when American labor unions grew stronger, stable employment became more common; as the proportion of men who could provide adequately for a family rose, the underclass shrank. Now it is growing again. As far as I can see, the only way to reduce its size would be to create and nourish both a business culture and labor unions that put as much weight on social solidarity and economic stability as on short-run efficiency. But labor leaders are the only Americans with any political influence who currently talk in these terms, and when they make such speeches nobody listens. Almost everyone else believes that efficiency (often called "competitiveness") must come first, and that social stability will somehow follow. How anyone can still believe this after watching what happened during the 1980s I do not know, but most people do.

Indeed, some economists still think America's problem is too much government regulation rather than too little. They believe unskilled workers would have a better chance of finding steady employment if we lowered the minimum wage. There is some evidence that lowering the minimum wage does create more low-wage jobs. But that is not the same as creating more stable jobs in which workers come to care about the enterprise that employs them or take some pride in doing useful work. Nor is there any guarantee that creating more low-wage work will reduce long-term joblessness. The real value of the minimum wage fell by a third during the 1980s. That may well have boosted employment. But long-term joblessness also rose, at least among men.

Many of the men who are now homeless would have a good chance of finding steady jobs if, as in World War II, unemployment stayed close to zero for a protracted period. Indeed, many would probably find steady jobs if unemployment stayed below 4 percent for a number of years. But that has not happened since 1945, and economists of all political persuasions agree that it would lead to an unacceptable level of inflation. That being the case, we need stopgap measures.

The best short-run solution to these workers' problems would probably be a day-labor market organized under public auspices. Everyone who wanted a day's work would show up at an early hour. If no private employer hired them, they would be entitled to public employment cleaning up parks or public buildings, or doing whatever else the community wanted done. In return, they would get vouchers for a cubicle hotel and three meals, plus a dollar or two for spending money. Assuming cubicles worth $8 a night, meals worth another $8, and $2 in cash, four hours of work should entitle anyone to room and board for the day. Those who wanted better accommodations, better food, or a bit more cash should be able to work longer and get more generous vouchers.

Many Americans will balk at bringing back the cubicle hotels, on the grounds that no affluent society should require anyone to live in such conditions. Cubicles without windows strike most people (including me) as particularly noxious. But a regular SRO room currently rents for almost twice as much as a cubicle. If we try to offer homeless adults a full-size room with a window and a private bath, as some nonprofit groups have, we will almost inevitably repeat HUD's experience with low-income families, providing good housing for a few and nothing for the majority. This does not mean we should accept cubicle hotels as the last word in low-income housing. It just means we should proceed incrementally. What the homeless need right now is some private space, however small, from which they can exclude others. Once they all get that, we can begin worrying about windows, floor space, private bathrooms, and kitchens.

We also need to remember that whatever housing entitlement we adopt for the homeless must be available to everyone else as well. Otherwise, we will create both perverse incentives and egregious inequities. Twenty-three million unmarried working-age adults lived in someone else's home in 1990. My best guess is that five million of them would move out if they had had more money.[12] If they could get an attractive permanently subsidized room by declaring themselves homeless, a fair number would probably do so. Another fourteen million unmarried working-age adults lived alone in 1990. Some would almost certainly be willing to get evicted if that would qualify them for a permanent rent subsidy in a nice place. Faced with numbers of this kind, even those who would like to give everyone an SRO room should think incrementally.

One big obstacle to guaranteeing everyone a cubicle in return for a few hours of work is that almost all the cubicle hotels in which we once housed the very poor are gone. That means we would have to convert existing shelters, warehouses, or other buildings. This need not be very expensive, as long as the goal is merely to give everyone a small private space of their own. But for this to happen most cities would need to rethink the municipal codes that currently govern such places. These codes were mostly written at a time when poverty was supposed to be on its way out. Since that hope has been disappointed, cities need new rules that will keep cheap housing within poor people's reach. That means keeping regulation to a bare minimum, focusing on things that have a demonstrable impact on fatal fires or the spread of contagious diseases. We also need to remember that the right question about a proposed cubicle hotel is not how it compares to an SRO but how it compares to the shelters and public places in which the very poor are now housed.

Another obstacle to creating such hotels is that no neighborhood wants them. Neighborhood groups will always be able to block private entrepreneurs' efforts to create "substandard" housing for the very poor, because they will be able to portray such entrepreneurs as cutting corners to make more money. That means private landlords can only create cheap rooms if they do it covertly. Churches and other nonprofit groups could sponsor cubicle hotels if these were defined as up-scale shelters charging a nominal fee, but even with altruistic sponsorship neighborhood opposition would persist. Most Americans want the homeless off the streets, but no one wants them next door.

One way to solve this so-called NIMBY ("not in my back yard") problem is to locate cubicle hotels in currently nonresidential areas. Such areas cannot be too isolated or nobody will be able to get to them. But if we could recreate skid row in relatively accessible areas, the poorest of the poor would at least have a place where they could legitimately be. Advocacy groups seldom support this approach, which they rightly characterize as an effort to ghettoize the poor. But we should not let idealism become the enemy of more modest improvements. For people who now live in congregate shelters, a nice room in a residential neighborhood is good ideal, but almost certainly not an attainable one. A cubicle in a nonresidential area is a far less inspiring ideal, but it is an attainable first step.

The Moral Contract

It is not clear how many of the homeless would be willing to work four hours a day for a cubicle and three cheap meals. Unlike today's shelters, a cubicle hotel would give single adults a private space with a lock on the door, accessible at any time, where they could leave their possessions and get mail and telephone messages. Some would judge that worth four hours of work. Others would not.

But even if some of the homeless refused such an offer, that would not be an argument against making it. Few Americans believe their society has an obligation to feed and house everyone, regardless of how they behave. When people act selfishly, taking advantage of those around them, Americans are quite willing—indeed eager—to see them suffer. But most of us do feel an obligation to help people who either cannot help themselves or are trying to do so and simply need an opportunity. Most Americans also know that some of the homeless fit this description, though they have no idea how large the proportion is. They badly want some way of distinguishing those who have a claim on society from those who do not. Offering everyone work is the most obvious test.

The difficult question is how much we can require of those who seek work. Must workers be sober? Must they refrain from using drugs on the job? Must they be able to remember what they have been asked to do? Must they actually apply themselves to the task at hand? Can they be fired? If workers can be fired, should the standards be those a private employer would use? If the public sector is to use the same standards as the private sector, does that mean the standards private firms use when unemployment is 3 percent or the standards they use when it is 7 percent?

My instinct is that a public day-labor market should ask as much as the private sector asks in normal times. If a public day-labor market tolerates malingerers, malingering will soon become the norm, little useful work will get done, and the voters will soon weary of the whole charade. I also think we should offer workers who perform unusually well a chance at better public-sector jobs with somewhat higher wages. With luck, these jobs could serve as gateways to steady employment in the private sector, by certifying a worker's diligence.

Helping the Mentally Ill

Finally, we come to the large minority of homeless adults with physical or mental disabilities that make them unemployable in the private sector. Many countries give such people sheltered employment of various kinds. If we are unwilling to do that, we should at least improve their disability benefits. At present, we have a two-tier system. Those who become disabled after they reach working age get relatively generous benefits from Social Security Disability Insurance. Those who become disabled before they are old enough to work must settle for Supplemental Security Income, which is far less generous. Although this system follows bureaucratic logic, it makes no moral sense. ssi for the mentally ill, who need supervision as well as room and board, should surely be more generous.

If we want to keep the mentally ill off the streets, we also need to correct two other failings of the current disability system. First, we have to stop assuming that the mentally ill will voluntarily set aside most of their monthly disability check for rent. Many are substance abusers, and even those who are not often act impulsively. If we want the mentally ill to remain housed, we should split their benefits into a rent voucher that they give to their landlord and a check that provides pocket money. Some places already do this. Vouchers not only help keep the mentally ill housed but increase their chances of getting medical care and social services. At present, the mentally ill often get completely lost because they have no fixed address at which their family, the mental-health system, or the postal service can find them.

We also need to alter our system of out-patient care to take account of the fact that room and board costs more for patients who are hard to live with. Some of the mentally ill can apparently get room and board for $500 a month. Some could not get anyone to house them even if they had a voucher worth $2000 a month. Rather than adopting a "one size fits all" approach to disability benefits, states need to provide more generous housing vouchers to out-patients who need more supervision. States also need to provide more financial support to families that care for severely disturbed relatives.

So long as the mentally ill stay housed and keep people informed of their whereabouts, they should be free to leave housing they find unsatisfactory. They should also get outside help with their housing problems, which can often be resolved fairly easily if a social worker or advocate intervenes early. But even if we do all this, a few patients will still end up on the streets. One will decide that her landlord is trying to poison her. Another will be evicted for threatening his neighbors. A third will simply vanish without leaving a forwarding address. If we want to eliminate *all* homelessness among the mentally ill, we will have to supplement housing subsidies and social workers with occasional coercion. That means rethinking the question of involuntary commitment.

One possible starting point is to reconsider what it means to say that patients should be locked up only when their behavior poses a danger to themselves or others. Rather than just asking whether mental patients are consciously suicidal, we might want to ask whether they should be free to select a way of life that will kill them. Living in the streets shortens people's lives. So does constant use of alcohol or cocaine. When people of sound mind harm themselves in these ways, we are rightly reluctant to intervene. But when the mentally ill make equally myopic choices, I think we have somewhat more obligation to intervene. That is especially true when self-destructive behavior is episodic rather than continuous. The strongest argument for coercion is that we have an obligation to protect everyone's better self from the darker forces that sometimes rule them. When all is darkness and there is nothing better left to protect, coercion is harder to justify.

I do not believe that anyone, sane or mad, has a constitutional right to sleep in the street. But that does not necessarily mean we should start locking up every mental patient who tries to do so. This is a problem that requires experimentation rather than appeals to principle. A plausible case can certainly be made for sending patients who cannot cope with conventional housing or a board-and-care facility to a hospital. It is true that many of these hospitals were once dreadful places, and some still are. But that does not necessarily mean they are worse than bus stations or doorways.

Coercion sometimes does more harm than good. But those who flinch from forcing the mentally ill to live in places intended for the purpose should recognize that their scruples have political costs. Only a tiny minority of the mentally ill will refuse to live in any form of conventional housing. But a much larger minority will sooner or later reject the particular housing that society offers them, especially if this housing has rules against drugs, alcohol, or troublesome behavior. When funds are limited, states will find it convenient to let such people leave and say they have "chosen" to live in the streets.

What happened when we gave the mentally ill the right to leave state hospitals in the late 1970s should serve as a warning. Once the courts forced state hospitals to let mental patients leave even if they had nowhere else to go, states soon converted this right into an obligation and began evicting patients who did not especially want to leave and had nowhere to go. Housing programs for the mentally ill might well do the same thing if we give patients a legal right to live in the streets. Eliminating that right may be the only practical way of forcing states to find housing for every mental patient.

What about Services?

Housing programs cannot solve most of the problems afflicting the homeless. Stable housing and daily work might reduce alcohol and drug consumption a little and might make some of the mentally ill a little saner, but they will not work miracles. The main benefit of housing is that it gives people a place to live. Almost everyone who deals with the homeless believes that they also need help with job skills, alcohol, drugs, depression, schizophrenia, and a host of other ills. If we knew how to solve these problems, doing so would be far more useful than creating dead-end jobs or makeshift housing.

Unfortunately, programs that try to improve people's skills, modify their chemical intake, or deal with their psychoses have rather mixed records of success. Changing people is hard, and doing it on a large scale is harder. Sometimes such programs work wonderfully well, but even when this is the case we seldom know why. When we try to clone successful programs, they often flop. Often it seems as if a particular individual makes all the difference. That is not a principle one can build into public funding. So service providers just keep asking for more resources, hoping that sometimes they will get it right.

The problem with services for the poor is not, as some cynics claim, that they never help. The problem is that we seldom know which ones are helping. That means we need to rethink our approach to evaluating such services. Two possible strategies deserve consideration: performance contracting and vouchers.

The idea behind performance contracting is simple: service providers should be paid more when they do a good job. If providers worked for contingent fees, getting paid a lot when their clients did unusually well and getting paid nothing when their clients did badly, even Republicans might support their requests for more money. When that is not the case, even Democrats are rightly cautious. The main obstacle to performance contracting is that performance is hard to measure, and whatever measures we emphasize soon become ends in themselves.

The idea behind vouchers is to make the homeless themselves more responsible for evaluating the services we offer them. When professional experts sell job training, alcohol abuse programs, or psychotherapy on the open market, the government usually assumes that clients can evaluate these services for themselves. If clients do not think they are getting their money's worth, they stop paying. If they think they have been defrauded, they can sue. But when the government offers such services to the poor, it seldom gives clients the right to shop around for the best program they can find. Instead, it gives money to the providers and sends them clients. Sometimes the clients never show up, suggesting that they do not think they are getting anything of value. But we seldom know whether that means the clients do not want help or merely that they do not want the kind of help they have been offered. If we gave the homeless vouchers for such services, we would no longer have to spend much on services that the homeless themselves judged worthless, and results might improve somewhat.

Neither performance contracting nor vouchers is a panacea. But in an era when everyone doubts the value of government programs, it is idle to expect that legislators will support high levels of public spending for programs organized in the traditional way. Nor do I think legislators ought to spend much on such programs until we have settled the homeless into more stable housing and improved our methods for deciding whether other services are effective.

Our dilemma, both as individuals and as a society, is to reconcile the claims of compassion and prudence. When I ponder that problem I often think of a homeless woman whom Elliot Liebow quotes at the end of *Tell Them Who I Am*.

"I'm 53 years old," Shirley says. "I failed at two marriages and I failed at every job I ever had. Is that any reason I have to live on the street?"

No government program is very likely to solve Shirley's marital or employment problems. But we can keep her off the street. Because we can, we should.

Appendices
Notes

Appendix 1:
Derivation of Tables 1 and 2

Derivation of Table 1

The estimates in Table 1 are derived from Martha Burt's 1987 survey of homeless adults in cities with 100,000 or more inhabitants. The data come from her *Over the Edge* (New York: Russell Sage, 1992); from her "Developing the Estimate of 500,000–600,000 Homeless People in the United States in 1987," in Cynthia Taeuber, ed., *Conference Proceedings for "Enumerating Homeless Persons: Methods and Data Needs,"* Bureau of the Census, March 1991; and from unpublished tables which she was kind enough to send me in answer to my questions. Burt drew random samples of potentially homeless respondents in shelters, soup kitchens, and congregating sites used by the homeless. These respondents were screened for homelessness using the criteria described in Chapter 2. Burt weighted respondents interviewed in shelters and soup kitchens to make them representative of all persons using services during the course of a week. I then used homeless respondents in congregating sites to estimate the proportion of the entire homeless population that did not use services.

My calculations use the following notation:

H   Total number of homeless individuals in cities of 100,000 or more in March 1987.

S   Number of homeless adults who used either a shelter or a soup kitchen at least once during the survey week ("service users").

N Number of homeless adults who used neither a shelter nor a soup kitchen during the survey week.

C Number of homeless children accompanying adults.

M_c Number of homeless adults accompanied by both a spouse and children.

M_{nc} Number of homeless adults accompanied by a spouse but no children.

P Number of homeless adults accompanied by children but no spouse.

L Number of homeless adults not accompanied by children or a spouse but accompanied by some other adult.

A Number of homeless adults not accompanied by anyone.

We know by definition that:

$$H = S + N + C. \tag{1}$$

In "Developing the Estimate." Burt reports that in congregating sites $S = .68(S + N)$. That yields:

$$N = .471S. \tag{2}$$

In "Developing the Estimate." Burt reports that all homeless adults in congregating sites who said they were accompanied by children also said they had used a shelter or a soup kitchen during the previous week. In *Over the Edge* (table 2-1), Burt reports that 1.3 percent of all homeless service users were accompanied by both children and a spouse. Another 8.6 percent were accompanied by children but no spouse. Adults accompanied by children reported an average of 2.2 children apiece (*Over the Edge*, p. 16). Since married couples are counted twice:

$$C = (2.2)(.013/2 + .086)S = .204S. \tag{3}$$

Substituting equations 2 and 3 into 1 we get:

$$H = S + .471S + .204S = 1.675S. \tag{4}$$

It follows that:

$$C = .122H \tag{5}$$

and

$$S = .597H. \tag{6}$$

Assuming that married adults with children (M_c) all use services and that they constitute 1.3 percent of all service users, then:

$$M_c = .013S = (.013)(.597H) = .008H. \tag{7}$$

Likewise, for single parents:

$$P = .086S = (.086)(.597H) = .051H. \tag{8}$$

We also know by definition that the homeless population can be divided into adults with children and spouses (M_c), adults with children but no spouses (P), children (C), adults with spouses but no children (M_{nc}), adults with neither children nor spouses but accompanied by other adults (L), and adults who are alone (A). Thus:

$$H = M_c + P + C + M_{nc} + L + A. \tag{9}$$

Since

$$M_c + P + C = .008H + .051H + .122H = .181H, \tag{10}$$

it must be the case that:

$$M_{nc} + L + A = .819H. \tag{11}$$

In *Over the Edge* (table 2-1) Burt presents data indicating that 2.4 percent of homeless service users were married couples not accompanied by children and that 6.5 percent were single adults accompanied by another adult but no children. Burt does not report analogous figures for adults who did not use services, so I assumed that their social arrangements were like those of service users not accompanied by children.

Since 9.9 percent of adult service users were accompanied by children, $2.4/(100 - 9.9) = 2.7$ percent of adult service users not accompanied by children were accompanied by a spouse, $6.5/(100 - 9.9) = 7.2$ percent were accompanied by some other adult, and the remaining 90.1 percent were alone. It follows that:

$$M_{nc} = (.027)(.819H) = .022H, \tag{12}$$

$$L = (.072)(.819H) = .059H, \text{ and} \tag{13}$$

$$A = (.901)(.819H) = .738H. \tag{14}$$

The estimated percentage in shelters on any given night comes from the calculations used to produce Table 2. For families with children, equations 15 and 20 show that $St/Sh_c = .016$ and $CH/(St + Sh)_c = .028$. Algebraic manipulation then shows that 95.8 percent of homeless families are in shelters on a given night. For single adults, equations 18 and 19 give us $St/Sh_a = 1.826$ and $CH_a/(St + Sh) = .031$. From this it can be shown that 34.3 percent of single adults are in shelters on any given night.

Derivation of Table 2

The 1980 shelter estimate. My estimate of the 1980 shelter population is based partly on the Census Bureau's 1980 count of "mission" residents and partly on combining HUD's 1984 shelter survey with Burt's estimate of the rate at which shelters added beds during the early 1980s.

The Census Bureau's 1980 shelter count was 23,000. (This figure comes from a letter to the General Accounting Office drafted by the Census Bureau for the signature of Undersecretary of Commerce Robert Ortner, dated March 21, 1988. So far as I know, it does not appear in any Census publication.) This count differs from the 1984 and 1988 HUD estimates in several important respects.

1. The 1980 figure is based on a count rather than a sample survey, so it is not subject to random sampling error.
2. The 1980 figure excludes an unknown number of shelter residents who reported that they had a permanent address elsewhere, whereas the 1984 and 1988 estimates include all persons sleeping in shelters, for whatever reasons.
3. The 1980 figure does not include individuals or families whom cities sent to cheap hotels in order to keep them off the streets.
4. The 1980 count omits individuals who did not fill out a census form and return it to the shelter operator, whereas the 1984 and 1988 HUD estimates are based on shelter managers' estimates of their average nightly census. Since

roughly a third of all conventional households must be
followed up to get a completed questionnaire, this could
be a major problem.

In light of these difficulties, the true 1980 shelter count could have been
considerably higher than 23,000.

To check the validity of the 1980 Census count, I looked at Burt's
estimates of shelter growth during the early 1980s. She calculates that
the number of shelter beds in cities of more than 100,000 grew 41
percent between 1981 and 1983 (*Over the Edge,* table 7-2). No one
thinks there was much growth during 1980 or 1981. Growth could have
been somewhat faster in cities of less than 100,000, but conventional
wisdom holds that homelessness grew mainly in large cities during the
early 1980s and spread to smaller cities later in the decade. Thus if
Burt's bed counts are accurate, it is hard to see how the national supply
of shelter beds could have grown by much over 50 percent between
March 1980 and January 1984.

Since HUD estimated that the nation had 100,000 shelter beds in
January 1984, a 50 percent growth rate implies that at least 66,000 beds
existed in 1980. Shelter operators told HUD that 70 percent of their
beds were occupied on an average night in January 1984. Operators
complained far more about overcrowding in 1984 than in 1980, so it
seems likely (though far from certain) that their 1980 occupancy rates
averaged less than 70 percent. But even if the 1980 occupancy rate was
as low as 50 percent, we still get an estimated nightly census of 33,000
people. A 60 percent occupancy rate would imply that 40,000 people
were in shelters on an average night.

These calculations leave a wide range of uncertainty. The 1980
shelter population was at least 23,000, but it could have been as high
as 50,000. I am fairly confident that it was between 30,000 and 40,000.
I picked 35,000 as the "most likely" value. Since separate shelters for
families with children were almost unknown in 1980, I assumed that all
35,000 shelter residents were single adults.

The 1984 and 1988 shelter estimates. My estimates of the 1984 and
1988 shelter population are based on HUD's sample surveys of shelter
operators. The 1988 survey covered shelters, "transitional" housing, and
hotels and motels paid for with vouchers for the homeless, but not

runaway shelters. The 1984 survey did not cover voucher programs, but these were still relatively rare in 1984, so omitting them should not affect my estimates much.

The 1988 survey covered cities of 25,000 or more, while the 1984 survey was confined to cities of 50,000 or more. HUD has estimated the relationship between the shelter population and city size in both years and used this relationship to estimate the number of shelter residents in the nation as a whole. (I took both the 1984 and the 1988 data from HUD's "1988 National Survey of Shelters for the Homeless," 1989.) Both surveys are subject to sizable sampling errors.

Both the 1984 and 1988 surveys asked shelter managers to estimate the number of individuals they had sheltered on an average night during a specified period. The 1984 survey asked about the month before the survey (January). The 1988 survey asked about the twelve months before the survey (September 1987 through August 1988).

The 1990 shelter count. The 1990 Census "S-night" count found 168,000 individuals in emergency shelters and hotels costing less than $12 a night, 10,000 in runaway and children's shelters, 12,000 in shelters for abused women, and 50,000 "visible on the streets." To maintain consistency with HUD's earlier surveys, I excluded runaway shelters but retained shelters for battered women. The 1980 count had found 28,000 people in hotels costing less than $4, but Census staff are convinced that cheap hotels account for a negligible fraction of the 1990 S-night total. I therefore assumed that only 10,000 of those counted were in cheap hotels, leaving 170,000 in emergency shelters and battered women's shelters.

If we exclude runaway shelters, S-night counted 28,770 children under the age of eighteen in emergency shelters and 5,615 in battered women's shelters, for a total of 34,385. Assuming a mean family size of 2.2 children and 1.1 adults, we get 51,578 members of homeless families with children. That leaves 118,000 childless adults.

The nonshelter-to-shelter ratio in 1987. What I call the nonshelter-to-shelter ratio (St/Sh) is the ratio of homeless persons sleeping in public places, institutions (jails, hospitals, detox centers), and unknown locations to homeless persons sleeping in shelters. Public places include public buildings, abandoned buildings, doorways, streets, parks, subway stations and tunnels, automobiles, and other places not intended for human habitation. The count of persons in jails, hospitals, and detox

centers does not include those who slept in these institutions throughout the week, since they would not have been available for interviewing
at a shelter, soup kitchen, or congregating site.

Burt provided me with tables showing where both her sample of
service users and her sample of nonusers in congregating sites had "slept
or rested" in the past twenty-four hours. The tables for service users
were weighted to represent all homeless adults who used services at any
time during the survey week. I assumed that the nonusers found in
congregating sites were representative of all nonusers.

All homeless adults in congregating sites who said they were
accompanied by children had used either a shelter or a soup kitchen
within the past week. My estimates for families with children are
therefore based on Burt's sample of service users. Among adult service
users accompanied by children, 91.6 percent had slept in a shelter or a
hotel paid for with vouchers the night before the interview; 6.2 percent
had slept in someone else's home or in a hotel paid for with their own
money; 1.5 percent had slept in a motor vehicle; and 0.7 percent were
unaccounted for. My estimate of the nonshelter-to-shelter ratio for
families with children (St/Sh_c) in 1987 is thus:

$$St/Sh_c = 1.5/91.6 = .016. \tag{15}$$

Among service users not accompanied by children, Burt's tables
show that 49.4 percent had spent the night before the interview in a
shelter or in a hotel paid for with vouchers. Another 8.0 percent had
spent the night in what I will call conventional housing (someone else's
home or a hotel paid for with their own money). That left 30.5 percent
who had spent the night in a public place and 12.1 percent whose
resting place could not be classified under any of these headings. For
my purposes, therefore, the nonshelter group is $30.5 + 12.1 = 42.6$
percent of the total. Those who had not used shelters or soup kitchens
during the week often gave more than one answer, apparently because
they moved around during the course of the night, but only 4.2 percent
said they had slept in conventional housing the night before the interview.

In order to combine service users and nonusers, I again assumed
that 32 percent of all homeless adults had not used services. Since 90.1
percent of service users were not accompanied by children, this assumption implies that $.32/([.68][.901] + .32) = 34$ percent of adults not

accompanied by children had not used services. On any given night, therefore, the proportion of all homeless adults not accompanied by children who slept in shelters (Sh/H_a) was:

$$Sh/H_a = (.66)(.494) = .326, \tag{16}$$

The proportion in public places (St/H_a) was:

$$St/H_a = (.66)(.426) + (.34)(.958) = .607. \tag{17}$$

The estimated nonshelter-to-shelter ratio for adults not accompanied by children (St/Sh_a) is thus:

$$St/Sh_a = .607/.326 = 1.862. \tag{18}$$

As a rough check on these calculations, I also looked at the 445 homeless adults found in congregating sites. Burt reports that 153 of these individuals initially said they had used a shelter within the past week; 103 initially said they had used a soup kitchen but not a shelter; 16 refused to answer; 31 of those who initially said they had not used a shelter or a soup kitchen turned out to have done so when interviewed in more detail; and 142 had used neither a shelter nor a soup kitchen. Assuming that the 31 who eventually proved to have used a shelter or a soup kitchen were like those who initially said they had done so, 40.1 percent of those who agreed to an interview had used a shelter at some point during the previous week.

Burt's data on service users suggest that those who used shelters during the survey week had spent an average of 4.3 nights in them. If the same were true of shelter users in congregating sites, $4.3/7 = 61.2$ percent of those who had used shelters at all would have used them the night before being interviewed. That would mean $(.401)(.612) = 24.6$ percent of those in congregating sites had used a shelter the night before being interviewed. If that were the case, the nonshelter-to-shelter ratio would be roughly $75.4/24.6 = 3.07$.

I suspect this figure is too high, because I am skeptical about the accuracy of Burt's data on shelter use over the previous week. Her data show that 34 percent of service users had used a shelter for seven nights; 18 percent had used a shelter for two to six nights; 24 percent had used a shelter only one night; and 24 percent had not use a shelter at all. The number of people who report using a shelter only one night, as against two or three, seems implausibly high, driving down the frequency of use figures for those who used shelters at all. My guess is that those who use shelters at all use them more like 80 percent of the time. That would imply a nonshelter-to-shelter ratio of 2.13, which is not too far from equation 18. I have no idea how many of the service users in congregating sites were accompanied by children.

Percent in conventional housing in 1987. Burt's definition of homelessness includes a few individuals who slept in conventional housing. In order to be included, such individuals had to be using a shelter or a soup kitchen or be in a congregating site for the homeless, and had to say either that they had no home or that they had no regular arrangement allowing them to stay in their current home at least five days a week. Although Burt's definition of homelessness is reasonable, it is somewhat broader than the one I employ elsewhere in this book. Table 2 therefore excludes those who had spent the past seven nights in conventional housing.

Burt's data on homeless service users show that 22 percent had spent at least one of the past seven nights in conventional housing and that 4 percent had spent all of the past seven nights in such housing. Those who had spent all seven nights in conventional housing accounted for 57 percent of those in conventional housing on any given night. Since 6.7 percent of all homeless single adults had spent the night before the survey in conventional housing, I assumed that $(1 - .57)(6.7) = 2.9$ percent of single adults were both homeless by my standards and in conventional housing on a randomly selected night. The ratio of homeless single adults in conventional housing (CH_a) to those in shelters and public places $(Sh + St)$ on a randomly selected night was:

$$CH/(Sh + St)_a = .029/(.494 + .426) = .031. \qquad (19)$$

Among families with children, 6.2 percent were in someone else's home the night before the interview. I assumed that 57 percent of them had been there throughout the previous week. Thus:

$$CH/(Sh + St)_c = (1 - .57)(.062)/(1 - .062) = .028. \qquad (20)$$

Changes in the Nonshelter-to-Shelter Ratio

An unpublished paper by Irwin Garfinkel and Irving Piliavin strongly suggests that the nonshelter-to-shelter ratio fell during the late 1980s.

("Homelessness: Numbers and Trends," Columbia University School of Social Work, 1994). They conducted a meta-analysis of local studies that either (a) counted all people sleeping in shelters and public places, or (b) counted all people in a sample of shelters and public places, or (c) asked homeless individuals sampled in different ways where they had spent the night. Surveys that try to count the homeless in public places are, in my judgment, almost certain to underestimate St/Sh. But that bias is not especially likely to change over time, so local studies can still tell us whether St/Sh has changed.

Garfinkel and Piliavin present estimates of the nonshelter-to-shelter ratio for all homeless individuals, regardless of whether they were members of families with children or single adults. I denote this as St/Sh. St/Sh is a weighted average of St/Sh_c and St/Sh_a. The number of homeless families rose much faster than the number of homeless single adults during the early 1980s. Since St/Sh_c is close to zero, while St/Sh_a is much higher, this compositional shift ensured that St/Sh would fall even if St/Sh_a remained constant. In practice, however, St/Sh falls too fast for that to be the only explanation.

Garfinkel and Piliavin's data cover a large number of different cities surveyed in different ways at different times. Nashville is the only city in their sample that conducted similar surveys year after year. That makes it tempting to argue that we should simply trust the Nashville data rather than trying to cobble together a time series based on different data and locations. That temptation is strengthened by the fact that St/Sh is roughly constant in Nashville, which makes estimation much easier. Nonetheless, Nashville is different from most American cities in two respects: its shelter population did not rise during the 1980s; and St/Sh was far lower in Nashville than in any other American city that did a similar survey during the early 1980s.

1980 through 1985. Garfinkel and Piliavin found no studies conducted before 1983, and they found no trend in St/Sh between 1983 and 1985. I therefore assumed that St/Sh_c and St/Sh_a were constant from 1980 through 1985.

1985 through 1990. If we set aside Nashville, seven of the eight studies conducted in 1983–1985 occurred during the summer, when St/Sh tends to be unusually high. Of these seven summer studies, six yielded estimates of St/Sh above 1.0, and four yielded estimates above

1.5. There were three summer studies in 1986–1989, which yielded slightly lower estimates of St/Sh. There were five summer studies in 1990–1992, which yielded values of St/Sh averaging around 0.5. A similar downward trend is apparent among winter studies.

As I have noted, the downward trend in St/Sh after 1985 is partly traceable to increased homelessness among families with children. If one calculates the overall nonshelter-to-shelter ratio using the values of St/Sh_c and St/Sh_a from equations 15 and 18 and the shelter populations in Table 2, the estimated value of St/Sh falls from 1.86 in 1980 to 1.51 in 1984 and 1.19 in 1987–88.

But compositional change is not sufficient to explain Garfinkel and Piliavin's findings. Their meta-analysis suggests that the natural logarithm of St/Sh fell by an average of 0.20 per year from 1983 through 1992. Compositional change lowered lnSt/Sh by $ln(1.51/1.19) = .24$ between 1984 and 1988, so about 30 percent of the overall decline in St/Sh is traceable to compositional changes. St/Sh_c has always been very low. The remaining decline in St/Sh must be largely traceable to declines in St/Sh_a. Table 2 assumes that lnSt/Sh_a fell by $(0.7)(0.20) = 0.14$ per year between 1985 and 1990.

The estimated value of St/Sh_a in March 1987 is 1.862. Since $ln1.862 = .622$, the implied March values of St/Sh_a for other years are:

March 1980 = $exp[.622 + (2)(.14)] = 2.464$
March 1984 = $exp[.622 + (2)(.14)] = 2.464$
March 1988 = $exp[.622 - .14] = 1.619$
March 1990 = $exp[.622 - (3)(.14)] = 1.224$

Because St/Sh_c is close to zero in Burt's data and because no one I talked with believed that it was much above zero even in the early 1980s, Table 2 assumes that it remained constant. I also assumed that the proportion of the homeless sleeping in conventional housing on a randomly selected night was constant.

Seasonal adjustments. The 1980 and 1990 Censuses and Burt's 1987 survey were conducted in March. The 1984 HUD survey was conducted in January. January is colder than March, but it is also dryer. At least in New York City, shelter use has been as high in March as in January. I therefore assumed that St/Sh was the same in January as in March.

The 1988 HUD survey asked shelter operators for average occupancy over the previous twelve months. Garfinkel and Piliavin's data suggest that St/Sh should be somewhat higher for the full year than for January or March. Extrapolating from their results, I assumed that St/Sh$_a$ for a full calendar year exceeded the March value by 0.20. My final estimates are thus:

	March 1980	Jan. 1984	1987–88	March 1990
St/Sh$_a$	2.464	2.464	1.819	1.224
St/Sh$_c$	NA	.016	.016	.016
CH/(St + Sh)$_a$	.031	.031	.031	.031
CH/(St + Sh)$_c$	NA	.028	.028	.028

Reconciling Table 2 with incidence estimates. Using these ratios and the shelter estimates given above, the total number of homeless adults appears to have been about 207,000 in 1984, 358,000 in 1987–88, and 289,000 in 1990. We can get a rough check on the validity of these estimates by looking at Bruce Link's 1990 telephone survey of adults in conventional households. (Link et al., "Reconsidering the Debate about the Size of the Homeless Population," paper presented at the October 1993 meetings of the American Public Health Association). Two-thirds of those contacted agreed to an interview. They were asked whether they had ever been homeless, whether they had been homeless in the past five years, and whether they had stayed in a shelter, on the streets, or in someone else's home when they were homeless. For clarity, I refer to those who had stayed in a shelter or on the street as "literally homeless."

Of those interviewed, 3.1 percent said they had stayed in a shelter or a public place within the past five years. If the rate were twice as high in households without telephones, the overall national rate would be 3.3 percent. (The Census Bureau estimates that 93.3 percent of American households had a telephone in 1990 [*Statistical Abstract, 1992,* table 884].) That would mean 5.9 million adults who had been literally homeless returned to conventional housing between 1985 and 1990. If the number of homeless adults grew by about 100,000 during this period (see Table 2), the number becoming homeless must have been 6.0 million, or 1.2 million a year.

Link also asked whether people had been homeless for less than a week, a week to a month, a month to a year, or more than a year. Because the mean spell for individuals in a given response category is uncertain, the mean for everyone who was homeless is also uncertain. Consider two alternative sets of assumptions:

Reported duration	Percent in group	Estimated mean (weeks) Low	High
Less than a week	8	.5	.5
Week to a month	33	2.0	2.5
Month to a year	46	12.0	28.0
More than a year	13	104.0	150.0
All	100	19.7	31.5

Most of those who reported being literally homeless had also lived in someone else's home during part of the time they were homeless. Thus if the average spell lasted 19.7 weeks overall, the average number of weeks spent in shelters and public places could in principle be far smaller—let us say 10 weeks. Conversely, if the average for all forms of homelessness was 31.5 weeks, the average number of weeks in shelters and public places could also be very high—let us say 26 weeks.

If 1.2 million adults became homeless each year and spent an average of 26 weeks in shelters and public places, 600,000 of them would have been literally homeless on any given night. If spells of literal homelessness averaged only 10 weeks, the nightly count would have averaged 230,000. Either estimate must be augmented by the (unknown) number of people who are permanently homeless and therefore missed by a survey like Link's.

Link's data are, then, potentially consistent with the estimates in Table 2, but they are also potentially consistent with much higher estimates. In order to resolve this uncertainty, we would have to survey a much larger sample of households and collect more detailed data from those who had been homeless, both on where they had stayed and how long they stayed there.

Appendix 2:
Supplementary Tables

Table A.1 Mentral Patients in State Hospitals, 1950–1990

	1950	1955	1960	1965	1970	1975	1980	1985	1990
Persons aged 15 and over (in millions)	109.5	116.3	125.6	135.6	148.2	162.5	174.1	184.8	196.8
Persons in state mental hospitals (in thousands)									
Expected[a]	512.5	544.3	588.1	634.8	693.8	760.8	814.8	865.1	921.1
Actual	512.5	558.9	535.5	475.2	337.6	193.4	132.2	109.9	92.1
Difference	0	−14.6	52.6	159.6	356.3	567.4	682.7	755.2	829.0
Hospitalization rate per 100,000 persons aged 15 and over	468	481	426	350	228	119	76	59	47

Source: Mental patients from David Mechanic and David Rochefort, "Deinstitutionalization: An Appraisal," *Annual Review of Sociology*, 16 (1990), 307. The 1990 estimate was provided by NIMH. Population estimates from Current Population Reports, "Money Income of Households, Families, and Persons in the United States, 1991," table B-14, and earlier editions.

a. Based on the 1950 ratio of persons in state mental hospitals to persons aged 14 and over.

Table A.2 Persons in One-Room Rental Units: Estimates from the Decennial Census (Numbers in 1000s)

Type of unit	1960	1970	1980	1990
One-room house or apartment	1128	974	1091	1058
Incomplete plumbing[a]	794	387	193	56
Gross rent below $150 in				
1989 dollars	544	310	230	125
Hotels, motels, rooming houses, Ys	641	322	204[b]	322[c]
Total	1769	1296	1295	1195[d]

Sources: Except where indicated, all data are from 1/1000 public-use samples of Census records and may differ slightly from published totals for the full Census.

a. Complete plumbing includes hot and cold running water, a shower or tub, a flush toilet, and a basin. In 1960 and 1970 these facilities had to be for the exclusive use of the tenant but could be located elsewhere in the building (e.g., at the end of a common hall); starting in 1980 they had to be in the tenant's own dwelling unit. In 1990 the "exclusive use" test was dropped.

b. *1980 Census of Population: Persons in Institutions and Other Group Quarters* (1984), table 43, reports that 176,000 people with no other permanent address lived in rooming houses, hotels, motels, or Ys charging $4 or more per night and that 51,000 lived in "low cost transient quarters." The latter category included both hotels and rooming houses charging less than $4 a night and free missions. A letter prepared by the Census Bureau for the signature of Undersecretary of Commerce Robert Ortner and sent to the General Accounting Office on March 21, 1988, indicates that 23,000 of these individuals were in missions. That leaves 28,000 in places charging less than $4 a night. The total number in rooming houses, hotels, motels, and Ys is thus 176,000 + 28,000 = 204,000.

c. This estimate, supplied by Denise Smith of the Census Bureau, excludes persons in hotels and rooming houses charging less than $12 a night. The Bureau has not, and apparently cannot, produce separate 1990 counts for shelters and cheap hotels. I assumed the figure was 10,000. This estimate is based partly on the 1989 AHS and partly on the conviction of Bureau staff members whom I asked that very few of those counted on "S-night" were in cheap hotels. Based on the 1980 results, the figure could be a bit higher.

d. Includes an estimate of 10,000 individuals in hotels and rooming houses costing less than $12 a night (see note c).

Table A.3 Observed and Quality-Adjusted Rents for All Tenants, Unsubsidized Tenants, Low-Income Tenants, Unsubsidized Low-Income Tenants, and Tenants in One-Room Units, 1973–1989

Type of tenant	1973	1975	1977	1979	1981	1983	1985	1987
ALL TENANTS								
Observed mean	$331	$334	$353	$356	$373	$396	$418	$427
Quality-adjusted mean	331	328	347	350	359	377	388	394
UNSUBSIDIZED TENANTS								
Observed mean	348	354	376	385	404	428	457	464
Quality-adjusted mean	348	345	365	372	384	400	410	414
TENANTS WITH INCOME BETWEEN $1 AND $9,999								
Observed mean	230	243	254	255	270	285	298	295
Quality-adjusted mean	230	235	248	248	257	269	280	283
UNSUBSIDIZED TENANTS WITH INCOME BETWEEN $1 AND $9,999								
Observed mean	253	274	292	299	320	334	356	351
Quality-adjusted mean	253	258	274	277	288	297	300	296
UNSUBSIDIZED TENANTS IN ONE-ROOM UNITS								
Observed mean	225	218	237	247	260	262	294	294
Quality-adjusted mean	225	218	224	229	245	247	278	283
UNSUBSIDIZED SINGLE MOTHERS WITH INCOME BETWEEN $1 AND $9,999 AND NO OTHER ADULT IN HOUSEHOLD								
Mean rent	284	293	305	314	332	347	353	356
Quality-adjusted mean	284	284	308	309	321	330	325	333

Table A.3 (continued)

Source: American Housing Surveys for 1973–1975 and odd-numbered years from 1977 to 1989. The sample excludes unoccupied units, units occupied by tenants who paid no cash rent, and a small number of units with missing data on one or more of the housing characteristics used in the analysis.

The means shown are the geometric means (the antilogs of the mean of the logged values) of gross monthly rent (rent plus utility bills). Tenants' estimates of their 1989 utility bills were inflated by 14 percent to offset the effect of a change in the 1989 questionnaire (see "Consistent Measures of Rent Trends—The American Housing Survey: 1985–1989," Joint Center for Housing Studies, Harvard University, no date). Rents were converted to 1989 dollars using the 1982–83 fixed-weight price index for personal consumption expenditures, taken from the national income accounts.

Quality-adjusted means were estimated from a regression equation that used the logarithm of gross rent as the dependent variable. The independent variables were dummy variables for the survey year, the location, age and type of building, the total number of rooms and number of bathrooms in the rental unit, the availability and type of air conditioning, the type of heating system, the type of sewer (a proxy for population density), broken plaster, cracks in the ceiling, leaks, holes in the floor, whether the unit had a complete kitchen, and whether it had electrical outlets in every room. The estimates shown here were derived by adding the coefficient for the survey year in this equation to the 1973 mean and taking the antilog of the result.

Table A.4 Mean Monthly Income, Expenditure, and Rent Reported to the Consumer Expenditure Survey, 1972–73 and 1980–1990

Group and measure	Respondents who answered at least one major income question			Respondents who answered all income questions			
	1972–73	1980–81	1988–90	1980–81	1984–85	1986–87	1988–90
ALL TENANTS							
Gross rent	$356	$330	$396	$321	$358	$376	$391
Monthly income	$1851	$1678	$1853	$1719	$1788	$1756	$1816
Monthly expenditure	$1578	$1750	$1910	$1743	$1827	$1830	$1869
Rent as percent of income	19.2%	19.7%	21.3%	18.7%	20.0%	21.4%	21.5%
Rent as percent of expenditure	22.6%	18.9%	20.7%	18.4%	19.6%	20.5%	20.9%
TENANTS WITH ANNUAL INCOME BETWEEN $1 AND $9,999							
Percent of all tenants	26.9%	31.5%	26.6%	29.7%	28.8%	29.8%	27.1%
Gross rent	$240	$243	$263	$224	$236	$254	$256
Monthly income	$496	$475	$535	$505	$496	$490	$538
Monthly expenditure	$759	$842	$931	$742	$803	$820	$909
Expenditure as percent of income	153.0%	177.3%	174.0%	146.9%	161.9%	167.3%	169.0%
Rent as percent of income	48.4%	51.2%	49.1%	44.3%	47.6%	51.8%	47.6%
Rent as percent of expenditure	31.6%	28.9%	28.2%	30.2%	29.4%	31.0%	28.2%

Source: Tabulations by Judith Levine from Consumer Expenditure Survey data tapes prepared by John Sabelhaus. Columns 1–3 cover what the Bureau of Labor Statistics calls "complete income reporters"—a category whose meaning changed slightly between 1972–73 and the 1980s but which includes everyone who reported a "major" source of income. Columns 4–7 cover only those who answered all the income questions. Gross rent is the sum of rent and utilities. Expenditure includes the full price of consumer durables, regardless of how they were financed.

Notes

1. Counting the Homeless

1. The Census Bureau did try to count people who were visible between 2:00 and 4:00 A.M. in public places frequented by the homeless, but it did not ask them whether they were homeless. When interviewers do ask people who are visible on the streets at this hour where they live, at least half say they live in conventional dwellings. Furthermore, when surveys of the homeless ask people where they spent the previous night, only a minority of the "street" homeless indicate that they were literally on the streets. The Bureau did try to count people emerging from abandoned buildings later in the morning, but its coverage of such buildings appears to have been spotty.

If all these biases cancel one another, the Bureau's final "street count" could be more useful than it seems. If half the unsheltered homeless were visible in public places during the small hours of the morning and half the people visible in such places were homeless, for example, the street count would equal the number of homeless individuals sleeping outside shelters, even though many of the wrong people would have been counted.

2. Mary Ellen Hombs and Mitch Snyder, *Homelessness in America: A Forced March to Nowhere* (Washington: Community on Creative Non-Violence, 1982).

3. See "A Report to the Secretary on the Homeless and Emergency Shelters" (Washington: Office of Policy Development and Research, U.S. Department of Housing and Urban Development, 1984).

4. Snyder's response is quoted in Richard White, *Rude Awakenings: What the Homeless Crisis Tells Us* (San Francisco: Institute for Contemporary Studies, 1992), p. 3.

5. Ibid., p. 4.

6. Those who want the homeless count to exceed one million could produce such a figure in a more responsible way if they were to estimate the number of people who become homeless over the course of a year. As we shall see, this figure is quite likely to exceed a million.

7. Martha Burt (personal communication) reports that in her 1987 survey of individuals found in shelters and soup kitchens who said they were homeless, 34 percent said they had spent the past seven nights in a shelter, 18 percent said they had spent the past seven nights in public places (streets, parks, public buildings, abandoned buildings, automobiles, subway stations, and so on), and 4 percent said they had spent the past seven nights in a conventional dwelling. That left 46 percent who spent time in some combination of such locations. In addition, many of those who had spent all seven nights in shelters or in public places had moved from one shelter to another or from one kind of public place to another.

8. For a detailed discussion of this issue, see Kathryn Edin, "Surviving the Welfare System: How AFDC Recipients Make Ends Meet in Chicago," *Social Problems,* 38 (November 1991), 462–474; and Kathryn Edin and Christopher Jencks, "Reforming Welfare," in my *Rethinking Social Policy* (Cambridge: Harvard University Press, 1992).

9. Bruce Link, Ezra Susser, Robert Moore, Sharon Schwartz, Elmer Struening, and Ann Stueve, "Reconsidering the Debate about the Size of the Homeless Population," paper presented at the American Public Health Association, October 1993.

10. See Rossi's *Down and Out in America* (Chicago: University of Chicago Press, 1989), p. 91. Martha Burt, who directed the Urban Institute's 1987 survey of large American cities, also provided me with tables showing that 22 percent of the homeless service users she interviewed had spent at least one night in someone else's home during the week before the interview. She does not report the number who used cheap hotels.

2. Estimating the Increase

1. "The 1988 National Survey of Shelters for the Homeless" (Washington: Department of Housing and Urban Development, 1989), exhibit 1, presents national estimates for both 1984 and 1988. Appendix 1 discusses the data in more detail.

2. Bureau of the Census, *Statistical Abstract of the United States, 1992* (Washington, 1992), table 74; see also Release CB-91-117. The Bureau's shelter count was subject to two offsetting biases. On the one hand, some communities made special efforts to get the homeless into shelters on "S-night"

so they could be counted. On the other hand, some communities had incomplete shelter lists, and in some cases the Census Bureau failed to deliver or collect forms. Since this was a one-night count of a transient population, no followup was possible. My guess is that the net result was a small undercount.

3. In table 7-2 of *Over the Edge,* Burt reports a fourfold increase in the number of big-city shelter beds between 1981 and 1989. Shelter growth was faster in smaller cities and suburbs, so I would expect the national increase to be somewhat greater than the increase in large cities.

4. Jennifer Toth, *The Mole People* (Chicago: Chicago Review Press, 1993), pp. 39, 151.

5. The response rate averaged 96 percent in shelters and soup kitchens and 92 percent in congregating sites. The survey of service users identified 1704 homeless respondents. The survey of congregating sites interviewed 999 individuals, 445 of whom proved to be homeless and 142 of whom said they had not used a shelter or a soup kitchen within the past week. Burt weighted the sample of service users to make it representative of all individuals who used shelters or soup kitchens at any time during the week. To achieve this, she weighted respondents by the inverse of the frequency with which they used services. She did not try to weight respondents found in congregating sites by the inverse of the frequency with which they came to such sites, presumably because it would have been hard to tell respondents what sites they should include in their estimates.

6. People without a permanent place to stay need not be homeless in the usual sense of the word, but including such people seems reasonable if they are also currently staying in a shelter, using a soup kitchen, or spending time in places frequented by the homeless.

7. Burt was kind enough to provide me with tables from her survey showing that 76 percent of all homeless service users had spent at least one of the past seven nights in a shelter and that 18 percent had spent all of the past seven nights in a public place. That accounts for 94 percent of her sample. Another 4 percent had spent all of the past seven nights in someone else's home or in a hotel. That left 2 percent who had spent the previous week in some combination of public places, other people's apartments, and unclassifiable locations.

8. Since parents living outside shelters must always worry about having their children taken away from them, those who spent the night in a public place might have denied it. But even when interviewers scour public places during the early hours of the morning looking for the homeless, they hardly ever encounter families with children.

9. These estimates come from Irwin Garfinkel and Irving Piliavin, "Home-

lessness: Numbers and Trends" (New York: Columbia University School of Social Work, 1994).

10. This estimate is based on the assumption that the shelter population grew at a uniform rate between January 1984, when HUD did its first shelter survey, and September 1998, when HUD did its second survey. Using linear interpolation, I estimate that about 50,000 family members and 150,000 single adults were in shelters on an average night during March 1987. Applying the methods described in Appendix 1, the best estimate of the total shelter population is then 348,000.

11. In "Developing the Estimate of 500,000–600,000 Homeless People in the United States in 1987" (in Cynthia Taeuber, ed., *Conference Proceedings for "Enumerating Homeless Persons: Methods and Data Needs,* 170 Bureau of the Census, March 1991), Burt argues for a figure between 500,000 and 600,000. Using the numbers reported in her paper, I too put the total above 500,000 in the first two drafts of this book. Unfortunately, the estimates of the shelter population in Burt's paper are not internally consistent. Thus while I have relied on her survey to estimate the rate of shelter use, I have not relied on it to estimate the number of shelter users or service users.

12. Appendix 1 describes the derivation of these estimates.

13. Burt, *Over the Edge,* p. 18, presents data indicating that 48 percent of homeless big-city service users had been homeless for six months or more in 1987. If the homeless population is in approximate equilibrium, the typical respondent is halfway through his or her spell of homelessness. Thus if the median respondent has already been homeless for six months, the median spell will last twelve months. Had Burt's data also included adults who did not use services, the median spell would probably have been a bit longer.

14. Rossi, *Down and Out in America,* p. 93.

15. "1988 National Survey of Shelters for the Homeless," exhibit 1.

16. This estimate is based on HUD's estimate that 65,000 members of families with children were in shelters during 1987–88, combined with Burt's estimate that homeless families with children had an average of 2.2 children and that roughly a tenth of them had two parents, making mean family size about 3.3.

17. Garfinkel and Piliavin, "Homelessness: Numbers and Trends."

18. HUD's 1987–88 estimate of the shelter population has a 90 percent confidence interval running from 135,000 to 225,000. If the true figure were at the low end of this range, the apparent decline between 1988 and 1990 would be spurious. If HUD's 1988 estimate was too high, that would help explain another puzzle. In 1988, HUD estimated that there were 172,000 shelter beds in cities of more than 250,000 ("1988 National Survey of Shelters

for the Homeless," exhibit 3). Yet Burt's 1989 shelter survey, which was based on a census rather than a sample, found only 94,000 beds in such cities (*Over the Edge,* p. 130).

19. Donald Bogue, *Skid Row in American Cities* (Chicago Community and Family Study Center, University of Chicago, 1963).

20. Bogue's suggestion that 110 people spent the night in public places was based on "discussions with persons familiar with the area," not on a systematic search. His estimate could be off a bit either way, but it is consistent with an actual street count made in Philadelphia two years later by a group from the Temple University Medical School. At 4:30 on a Sunday morning in February, they interviewed everyone on the streets in Philadelphia's skid row. They found 64 men who "had spent the night walking the street or sleeping in all night restaurants." See Leonard Blumberg, Thomas Shipley, and Irving Shandler, *Skid Row and Its Alternatives* (Philadelphia: Temple University Press, 1973), pp. 230–232. If we allow for the fact that Philadelphia is a smaller city, this count is very close to Bogue's Chicago estimate.

3. Emptying the Back Wards

1. Rossi, *Down and Out in America,* p. 154.

2. Burt, *Over the Edge,* table 2-2.

3. Rossi, *Down and Out in America,* p. 169. Rossi also reports (p. 132) that 50 percent of the men and 71 percent of the women who were homeless in Chicago during 1985–86 said they had had at least one child.

4. This estimate is based on tables 6.5 and 6.6 in Rossi's *Down and Out in America* and is approximate.

5. The homeless also seem to have many other less dramatic mental problems that persist after they return to conventional housing. The one study I know that investigates what happens to the homeless after they return to conventional housing is Elliot Liebow's moving description of homeless women in suburban Maryland, *Tell Them Who I Am* (New York: Free Press, 1993).

6. Bogue (p. 207) reports that 9 percent of those living on Chicago's skid row in 1958 had serious mental problems and that another 9 percent had less serious mental problems.

7. This approach to estimating the size of the deinstitutionalized population implicitly assumes that the mental health of the adult population did not really change between 1950 and 1990. If mental health improved, Figure 1 exaggerates the size of the deinstitutionalized population; if mental health deteriorated, Figure 1 underestimates the size of the deinstitutionalized population.

8. The number of admissions to state hospitals does not seem to have

declined over time, but today's admissions probably involve more repeaters and fewer first-time patients than admissions forty years ago.

9. In table 7.3 of *Mental Hospitalization* (Newbury Park, Calif.: Sage Publications, 1987), Charles Kiesler and Amy Sibulkin show that the number of mentally ill nursing-home patients rose from 101,000 in 1964 to 148,000 in 1969; 273,000 in 1973; and 394,000 in 1977. In 1964 there were almost five times as many mentally ill patients in state hospitals as in nursing homes. By 1977 there were twice as many in nursing homes as in state mental hospitals. In addition, a large number of patients diagnosed only as senile shifted from mental hospitals to nursing homes.

10. This estimate is based on applying the age data in Table 4 to the total counts in Table 2.

11. In *Mental Hospitalization* (p. 189) Kiesler and Sibulkin summarize a series of studies that investigated the living arrangements of patients discharged from state hospitals in the 1960s and 1970s. About 70 percent went to live with relatives in both periods. In the 1970s, about 20 percent lived alone and 10 percent lived in group homes. In the early 1960s, about 15 percent lived alone and 15 percent lived in group homes. Given the many differences between the samples covered, the apparent shift from group homes to living alone should not be read as evidence of a trend.

12. Martell and Dietz, "Mentally Disordered Offenders Who Push or Attempt to Push Victims onto Subway Tracks in New York City," *Archives of General Psychiatry*, 49 (June 1992), 472–475.

13. The only study I know that tried to compare arrests for violent crime among the homeless and the conventionally housed covers Austin, Texas, in the early 1980s. To everyone's surprise, the authors found that the homeless were somewhat less likely than other citizens to be arrested for violence. See David Snow, Susan Baker, and Leon Anderson, "Criminality and Homeless Men: An Empirical Assessment," *Social Problems*, 36 (December 1989), 532–549.

While Austin was probably representative of southwestern cities in the early 1980s, it was quite different from major northern cities in the late 1980s. Sixty percent of the homeless men Burt interviewed in large cities said they had spent at least five days in jail, and 29 percent said they had spent time in a federal or state prison. We do not know how many of these individuals were arrested or served time for violent crimes, but the overall percentage was almost certainly higher than in the general population.

14. The federal component of SSI is indexed to inflation, but state supplements are not. Only two states raised these supplements enough to keep pace with inflation during the 1980s. About half the states currently supplement

federal SSI payments, but only Alaska, California, Connecticut, Massachusetts, and Wisconsin currently add more than $100 a month to the basic federal allotment.

15. See especially Burton Weisbrod, "A Guide to Benefit-Cost Analysis, as Seen through a Controlled Experiment in Treating the Mentally Ill," in A. Razin, E. Helpman, and E. Sadka, eds., *Social Policy Evaluation: An Economic Perspective* (New York: Academic Press, 1983). For a more general review of the evidence on out-patient versus in-patient care, see Kiesler and Sibulkin, *Mental Hospitalization*.

16. *Statistical Abstract*, 1993, table 195.

17. Ibid., *1993*, table 195, and *1987*, table 159. I converted current hospital budgets to constant dollars using the implicit price deflator for gross domestic product (GDP), not the price index for medical services. The price index for medical services rose much faster than the GDP deflator, so using it would imply a sharp drop in mental hospitals' real expenditures. But medical prices rose largely because of expensive technical innovations. No such innovations occurred in mental hospitals during these years, so estimating their costs on the basis of what happened to costs in other hospitals makes no sense.

A more plausible approach to estimating state mental hospitals' costs is to assume that labor productivity was constant and that, all else equal, their costs should have risen at the same rate as the average American worker's total compensation (wages plus fringe benefits). Labor Department statistics suggest that compensation per hour in the nonfarm business sector rose 152 percent between 1975 and 1990. Since staff size fell 20 percent, state mental hospitals' personnel expenditures would have risen 101 percent in the absence of other changes. State mental hospitals' total expenditures rose 141 percent in this period, but not all that money was for personnel.

18. For a good history of this debacle, see Howard Goldman and Antoinette Gattozzi, "Balance of Powers: Social Security and the Mentally Disabled," *Milbank Quarterly*, 66 (1988), 531–551.

19. See the General Accounting Office's followup summarized in House Committee on Ways and Means, *1991 Green Book*, pp. 65–67.

20. The number of disabled nonelderly SSI and SSDI beneficiaries rose from 4.78 million in 1980 to 5.46 million in 1989, with all the growth concentrated in SSI (*1991 Green Book*, pp. 63, 757). The number of people between the ages of twenty and sixty-four rose from 129.6 to 146.0 million. The fraction of such people receiving benefits was thus 3.68 percent in 1980 and 3.74 percent in 1989. The percentage of the working-age population collecting disability benefits rose even more during the Bush years.

21. Ibid., p. 66. Unfortunately, these figures cover only those new beneficiaries who have worked long enough to qualify for Social Security Disability Insurance, not those receiving SSI disability benefits.

22. This estimate covers persons between the ages of eighteen and sixty-four with mental illnesses that prevent them from holding a job of any kind (other than sheltered employment). It includes 100,000 people in mental hospitals; 100,000 in nursing homes; 100,000 who are homeless; 1.1 million in conventional households or board-and-care facilities who received federal benefits for a mental disability; and 300,000 to 500,000 in conventional households who did not receive federal benefits, for a total of 1.7 to 1.9 million.

The estimate for mental hospitals assumes that there were 143,000 persons in mental hospitals on an average day in 1987 (*Statistical Abstract, 1991*, table 167) and that 72 percent of them were between the ages of eighteen and sixty-four (a figure taken from unpublished Census Bureau tabulations for 1990).

The estimate for nursing homes assumes that the age distribution and diagnoses of nursing-home patients were the same in 1987 as in 1977, when 6.2 percent of all nursing-home residents were both under the age of sixty-five and suffering from mental illness or senility. See Howard Goldman, Judith Feder, and William Scanlon, "Chronic Mental Patients in Nursing Homes: Reexamining Data from the National Nursing Home Survey," *Hospital and Community Psychiatry*, 37 (March 1986), 269–272. I applied this ratio to the nursing-home count for 1986 (*Statistical Abstract, 1991*, p. 105).

The estimate for the homeless assumes that 400,000 people were homeless in 1987 (see Table 2), that 97 percent of them were under the age of sixty-five (Burt, *Over the Edge*, p. 14), that 12 percent were under the age of eighteen (see Table 1), and that 30 percent of homeless nonelderly adults had disabling mental illnesses at any given time.

The estimate for persons receiving federal benefits due to a mental disability who were under sixty-five and not living in institutions is extrapolated from data in the *1991 Green Book* (pp. 63, 738, 751, 757).

Since only 4 percent of the homeless got SSI (Burt, *Over the Edge*, p. 20), the number who both got benefits and were homeless appears to be negligible.

The estimate for persons in conventional households who were unable to work because of mental illness but got no federal benefits is a wild guess, based largely on what we know about subsequent rates of employment among those denied disability benefits. The number could be considerably higher.

23. *Statistical Abstract, 1993*, table 195, and *1987*, table 159.

24. The expenditure figure is based on combining Burt's data on per capita spending (*Over the Edge*, p. 125) with population estimates in *Economic Report*

of the President, 1993 (table B-25). Converting to 1987 dollars, I estimate that state spending on residential services for mental patients rose from $350 million in 1981 to $700 million in 1987. Note 22 suggests that 1.1 million deinstitutionalized patients were getting disability benefits for mental illness in 1987. The analogous figure for 1981 appears to have been about 1.0 million. Prorating total expenditure over all patients getting federal disability benefits and dividing by twelve yields the monthly figures in the text.

25. *1992 Green Book*, p. 791.

26. I do not have salary data for those who cared for the mentally ill, but the bulk of state hospital spending goes for salaries, and state hospitals' spending, measured in constant dollars, rose 19 percent between 1979 and 1990, while staff size fell more than 13 percent (*Statistical Abstract, 1993*, table 195, and *1987*, table 159).

4. The Crack Epidemic

1. There is no consensus on how to measure alcohol problems. Some investigators focus on the amount of alcohol respondents say they consume, while others are more interested in how often respondents report being drunk. Some investigators collect life histories and base their judgments on these histories. Others ask whether the respondent was ever in a residential treatment program for alcoholism. Needless to say, when we combine these variations in method with dramatic differences in the samples studied, the results are highly variable.

2. Eighty percent of those in general-purpose shelters for single adults tested positive for something. Among all single adults who tested positive, 83 percent had used cocaine. Urine was also tested for alcohol and marijuana, but their presence tells us relatively little about people. There was little evidence of drugs other than cocaine, alcohol, and marijuana. See Andrew Cuomo, chair, *The Way Home: A New Direction in Social Policy* (New York: New York City Commission on the Homeless, 1992), p. C-2.

3. Bureau of Justice Statistics, *Sourcebook of Criminal Justice Statistics, 1991* (Washington, 1992), p. 473.

4. I am indebted to Peter Rossi for providing me with these data, which come from the 1987 Urban Institute survey.

5. Rossi, *Down and Out in America*, p. 103.

6. For an ethnographic account that pushes this idea about as far as one can without being irresponsible, see David Snow and Leon Anderson, *Down on Their Luck: A Study of Homeless Street People* (Berkeley: University of California Press, 1993).

7. For a sympathetic but unblinking narrative that manages to capture both the similarities and the differences between the homeless and the rest of us, I recommend Liebow's *Tell Them Who I Am*.

5. Jobs and Marriage

1. For survey data describing the public's views on the causes of homelessness, see Barrett Lee, Bruce Link, and Paul Toro, "Images of the Homeless: Public Views and Media Messages," *Housing Policy Debate*, 2 (1991), 649–682.

2. Rossi, "The Precariously Housed in America: Demographic Sources of Homelessness" (Social and Demographic Research Institute, University of Massachusetts, Amherst, 1992). My approach differs from Rossi's only in its details.

3. This and subsequent income estimates for homeless single adults come from tabulations that Rossi made for me from Burt's original data.

4. Readers familiar with HUD's low-income housing programs will recognize that my definition of the low-income population bears no relationship to HUD's. Eligibility for HUD programs depends on family income rather than individual income. Families have low incomes if their income is less than 80 percent of the local median—a threshold that makes 38 percent of all households eligible for assistance. Families have "very low" income, and enjoy priority in some HUD programs, if their income is less than half the local median. This cutoff still includes 22 percent of all households. (See "Priority Housing Problems and 'Worst Case' Needs in 1989: A Report to Congress," Department of Housing and Urban Development, 1991, pp. 3–7.) This chapter focuses on individual rather than family income and sets a much lower threshold than HUD does. Using my definition, only 6 percent of working-age men and 17 percent of working-age women had extremely low incomes in 1989.

5. Although the data on income and weeks worked cover 1969, 1979, and 1989, the data on marital status are for March of the following year.

6. See my *Rethinking Social Policy*, pp. 165–166.

7. Ibid, fig. 5.5.

8. Among unmarried working-age men, long-term joblessness averaged 12.6 percent in 1969; 12.6 percent in 1979; and 13.7 percent in 1989. Among married working-age men it averaged 3.5 percent in 1969; 6.2 percent in 1979; and 7.7 percent in 1989. In a period when the rate for all men doubled, therefore, the rate for married men more than doubled.

9. *Rethinking Social Policy*, figs. 5.1 and 5.2.

10. Chinhui Juhn, "Decline of Male Labor Market Participation: The Role

of Declining Market Opportunities," *Quarterly Journal of Economics* (February 1992), 79–121.

11. The proportion of the long-term jobless with family incomes below the poverty line follows the same trajectory (*Rethinking Social Policy,* p. 159).

12. Throughout this book I write as if adults always reported their own incomes to the Census Bureau. In reality, the Bureau usually collects data on all members of a household from a single informant, who is usually the head or the spouse of the head. These informants are often poorly informed about the incomes of other people in their household. This fact probably exacerbates the general problem of underreporting.

13. See *Rethinking Social Policy,* table 4.1.

14. The estimates in the text are based on the data in Table 6.

15. Ibid.

16. See Edin and Jencks, "Reforming Welfare," in *Rethinking Social Policy.*

17. Between 1980 and 1990 the personal consumption expenditure deflator from the national income accounts rose 61 percent. Meanwhile, welfare benefits for a single mother with two children and no other reported income rose 26 percent in the median state. See House Commitee on Ways and Means, *1992 Green Book,* p. 645.

18. Ibid, p. 675.

19. The most influential statement of this position is William Julius Wilson, *The Truly Disadvantaged* (Chicago: University of Chicago Press, 1987). For a discussion of Wilson's argument, see chapter 4 of my *Rethinking Social Policy.*

20. For an assessment of both this view and Wilson's see Robert Mare and Christopher Winship, "Economic Opportunities and Trends in Marriage for Blacks and Whites," in Christopher Jencks and Paul Peterson, eds., *The Urban Underclass* (Washington: Brookings Institution, 1991), pp. 175–202.

21. See Jane Mansbridge, "The Role of Discourse in the Feminist Movement" (Evanston: Center for Urban Affairs and Policy Research, Northwestern University, 1993).

6. The Destruction of Skid Row

1. The decennial Census covers a much larger sample of one-room units, but it does not ask persons living in hotels or rooming houses how much monthly rent they pay. In 1980 and 1990 the Census also drew an arbitrary distinction between those hotels and rooming houses charging more than a specified amount ($4 a night in 1980, $12 a night in 1990) and those charging less. People living in hotels and rooming houses charging less than the specified

amount were grouped with persons living in free missions or shelters. This was true both in published counts and in the public-use data tapes.

2. The 1973–1983 samples include about 600 one-room units per year. The 1985–1989 samples include about 300 one-room units per year.

3. Interviewers had a set of definitions available if respondents asked what they should count, but they did not read these definitions unless respondents asked.

4. To avoid a flood of numbers, Table 7 shows data for only five years. I have examined identical tabulations for all the odd-numbered years from 1973 through 1989, and the results are consistent with the generalizations in the text.

5. The AHS sample is redrawn after each decennial Census. The sampling frame is then updated every year to include newly constructed units. Units are dropped when they are torn down or abandoned. The 1973–1983 AHS surveys were based on a sample drawn from the 1970 Census. The 1985–1989 surveys were based on a sample drawn from the 1980 Census. If updating worked perfectly, there would be no more difference between the 1983 and 1985 samples than between, say, the 1981 and 1983 samples. But updating procedures are never perfect, so the measured characteristics of the housing stock tend to change more when a new sample is drawn than when an old one is updated. In this case the Census Bureau drew a new sample in the same year that it changed the AHS questionnaire. There is no good way to separate the effects of the two changes.

6. The estimated number of tenants in hotels and rooming houses rose from 116,000 in 1985 to 127,000 in 1987 and then jumped to 162,000 in 1989. Without the 1991 data, it is impossible to decide how much of the increase between 1987 and 1989 was real.

7. In 1985–1989, only 27 percent of one-room rental units in hotels and rooming houses had a complete bathroom and only 9 percent had a complete kitchen. Among one-room rental units in conventional apartment buildings and converted single-family residences, in contrast, 87 percent had complete bathrooms and 69 percent had complete kitchens.

8. These estimates achieved wide circulation after they appeared in Ellen Baxter and Kim Hopper, "Shelter and Housing for the Homeless Mentally Ill," in Richard Lamb, ed., *The Homeless Mentally Ill: A Task Force Report of the American Psychiatric Association* (Washington: American Psychiatric Association, 1984), pp. 109–140. Baxter and Hopper took the figures from a useful paper by Cynthia Green, "Housing Single Low-Income Individuals." Green's data do not cover SROs in the usual sense of the term. She estimated the number of one-room and two-room units "lacking facilities" (such as a complete bath-

room) in the 1973 and 1979 AHS. There are far more two-room than one-room units.

9. See, for example, Hoch and Slayton, *New Homeless and Old,* p. 174.

10. The number of unmarried working-age men with incomes below $2500 shows no trend from 1974 through 1979. It rose from 2.5 million in 1979 to 3.3 million in 1980; 3.7 million in 1981; 4.7 million in 1982; and 4.9 million in 1983. After that the figure fell to 4.7 million in 1984; 4.5 million in 1985; 4.4 million in 1986; 4.3 million in 1987; 4.0 million in 1988; and 3.9 million in 1989. Since I adjusted incomes for inflation using the 1982–83 fixed-weight price index for personal consumption expenditures from the national income accounts, the sharp rise between 1979 and 1981 cannot be blamed on the well-known defects of the Consumer Price Index before 1983.

11. As we shall see in Chapter 8, the balance between cheap units and poor tenants is not necessarily a reliable guide to how much rent poor people pay, because the proportion of cheap units occupied by poor people also varies. In the case of one-room units, however, the correlation between tenants' income and rent did not change much between 1973 and 1989. Rent burdens therefore tell the same story as Figure 2.

12. The rents in the text are geometric rather than arithmetic means and exclude tenants who paid no cash rent, lived in public housing, or got a means-tested rent subsidy. Appendix Table A.3 gives both the observed and quality-adjusted means, along with details of the estimation procedure.

13. Not all individuals reporting incomes below $2500 were really surviving on that amount. In the late 1980s, for example, more than a third of those who lived in a single room and reported incomes below $2500 reported no income whatever. For lack of a better solution I have assumed that people living in single rooms underreport their cash incomes by the same amount as people who are homeless.

14. Donald Bogue, *Skid Row in American Cities* (Chicago: Community and Family Studies Center, University of Chicago, 1963).

15. I am indebted to William McAllister and Gordon Berlin for information about New York's lodging houses.

16. The overall Consumer Price Index rose by a factor of four during this period. The estimates in the text are based on data in *Economic Report of the President, 1992,* pp. 361–362; and Department of Commerce, *The National Income and Product Accounts of the United States: 1929–82, Statistical Tables* (Washington, 1986), table 7.10.

17. Using 1989 dollars, Census data for rental units other than hotels and rooming houses show that rents averaged $247 in 1960; $315 in 1970; and $365 in 1980. The 1989 AHS mean for such units is $423. The analogous

figures for one-room units are $173 in 1960; $236 in 1970; $276 in 1980; and $349 in 1989. All these figures include subsidized units, and none is quality-adjusted. All are arithmetic means, so they are not comparable to the geometric means or medians reported in my tables.

7. Social Skills and Family Ties

1. The rent estimate for a room in a nonrelative's home comes from the 1989 AHS and excludes individuals who paid no cash rent.

2. These are gross rents for AHS tenants in multiunit apartment buildings.

3. The data on the homeless come from Burt's *Over the Edge,* p. 29. The data for the general population come from the Current Population Survey.

4. The 1987 CPS found that 65 percent of working-age adults were living with a spouse. Burt (p. 15) found that only 4 percent of homeless adults who used services in big cities during 1987 were accompanied by a spouse.

5. All these estimates come from the March Current Population Survey data tapes.

6. Appendix Table A.1 shows that there were 481 patients in state mental hospitals per 100,000 persons aged fourteen and over in 1955. By 1975 the figure was down to 119 per 100,000.

8. Changes in the Housing Market

1. See Burt, p. 45, and Rossi, p. 182.

2. I used the 1982–83 fixed-weight price index for personal consumption expenditures (PCE), taken from the national income accounts, to measure overall price changes. This index measures changes in the price of the market basket that consumers purchased in 1982–83, which was roughly the middle of the period under investigation. Unlike the Consumer Price Index, which covers only urban consumers, the PCE index covers all consumers. Nonetheless, the PCE and the CPI tell similar stories. The revised Consumer Price Index (CPI-U-X1), which corrects errors in the official index's treatment of home-ownership costs during the 1970s, rose 163 percent between 1973 and 1989. The PCE index rose 158 percent. Using the CPI-U-X1, the median tenant's real income fell 3 percent between 1973 and 1989. Using the PCE index, it fell 1 percent.

The match between the periods covered by the AHS income data and by my PCE price data is imperfect. The AHS starts its interviewing in September and continues through the fall. It asks respondents about their income during the twelve months prior to the interview, so the typical respondent is probably reporting on income from October of the previous year through September of the current year, while reporting on rent in October of the current year. I used the PCE price index for the current calendar year.

Imperfect matching between income, rent, and price data leads to more serious problems in 1979 than in 1973 or 1989. Inflation was running close to 1 percent a month in 1979, so the 1979 price index probably underestimates tenants' monthly income at the time of the interview by about 6 percent. The downward bias is smaller in 1973 and 1989 because inflation was slower. Analogous problems arise when estimating changes in real rents, which are overstated in all years but especially in 1979.

3. Since other analysts emphasize the ratio of median rent to median income, I have done the same. This ratio moves in fits and starts, because both reported rents and reported incomes tend to cluster at values divisible by 10, 50, 100, and 1000. If one divides each family's rent by its income, the median of this distribution is slightly lower than the ratio of median rent to median income. It also changes more smoothly over time, rising from 0.203 in 1973 to 0.239 in 1979 and 0.264 in 1989.

4. I excluded tenants who reported no income or negative income (from business losses) from the low-income category. These tenants' median rent is much higher than that of other low-income tenants, suggesting that they have either savings or unreported income with which to pay their rent. Analyses that include such tenants yield almost identical conclusions.

5. Because of changes in the interview schedule, the data in Table 8 may slightly exaggerate the increase in low-income tenants' rent burden during the 1970s and understate the increase during the 1980s. Prior to 1989, some tenants who got rent subsidies reported their contract rent rather than the amount of rent they themselves paid. Because such tenants became more numerous during the 1970s, the effect of this bias probably grew. The 1989 questionnaire was revised in such a way as to make such errors less likely. This creates a very small downward bias in the trend estimates for the 1980s.

6. If one calculates individual rent-to-income ratios for low-income tenants, the median rose from 0.440 in 1973 to 0.490 in 1979, peaked at 0.573 in 1985, and then fell back to 0.515 in 1989. For those in unsubsidized units, the figures are 0.513 in 1973; 0.560 in 1979; 0.647 in 1985; and 0.649 in 1989.

7. The trend in vacancy rates shown in Table 8 should be treated with caution because of methodological changes between 1983 and 1985. The vacancy rate for low-rent units shows no clear trend from 1973 to 1983. Nor

is there a clear trend between 1985 and 1989. The rate was 8.2 percent in 1985; 9.9 percent in 1987; and 9.0 percent in 1989.

8. Those who see a shortage of affordable housing argue that many of the vacant low-rent units found in the AHS are not really available to tenants, because they are being abandoned. But in most cases abandonment is itself evidence of weak demand. Landlords who are losing money normally respond by raising rents until either (a) the building becomes profitable or (b) the vacancy rate gets so high that further rent increases seem likely to reduce rather than increase revenue. Only if this point is reached before the building becomes profitable will the landlord abandon it. One exception to this rule is that landlords may abandon buildings without vacancies if rent control holds their income below the breakeven point, but except perhaps in New York that is unusual. Another exception is that landlords will tear down buildings that have plenty of tenants if they can put the land to a more profitable use. But landlords who are planning to tear down a building seldom list their empty units as being for rent.

9. See Ira Lowry, "Inflation Indexes for Rental Housing" (Santa Monica: Rand Corporation, 1982).

10. Bureau of Justice Statistics, "Highlights from 20 Years of Surveying Crime Victims" (Washington, 1993).

11. Because of changes in the AHS questions about household composition between 1973 and 1974, I was unable to construct a 1973 sample of single mothers comparable to that for later years.

12. The AHS asks respondents about their income for the twelve months before the interview while asking about rent and utility bills at the time of the interview. If a family's income has risen recently, and if it has moved as a result, its current monthly rent could exceed its average monthly income for the previous twelve months. The 1989 AHS added new questions aimed at identifying households in which income had changed recently. Using these revised measures reduces the proportion of families with very high rent burdens, but the reduction is not dramatic.

13. For evidence that such situations are extremely common see Edin and Jencks, "Reforming Welfare," in my *Rethinking Social Policy.*

14. For subsidized tenants in private housing, the 30 percent limit may not include utilities. Gross rents between 30 and 50 percent of reported income are thus quite plausible for such tenants. In addition, HUD now has some programs in which it makes up the difference between 30 percent of the tenant's income and the local "fair market rent" but allows tenants to pay more than the fair market rent so long as they cover the excess themselves.

15. Roughly a third of all respondents fail to answer one or more of the

Census Bureau's income questions. When income data are missing, the Bureau substitutes the amount reported by the last previous tenant with similar characteristics. This procedure introduces a lot of random error in income measures, driving up the proportion of respondents with high estimated rent burdens. Matters are further complicated by the fact that some tenants apparently reported their total rent rather than the portion they actually paid. The questionnaire was clarified in an effort to eliminate such errors in 1989.

16. The estimates from the CES are based on tabulations by Judith Levine for unmarried female heads of families with children. All respondents were interviewed between 1980 and early 1990, lived in urban areas, rented their homes, answered all the income questions, remained in the survey for four quarters, and had positive incomes. Among those with reported incomes below $5000, mean annual expenditure averaged $720 a month in 1989 dollars, mean income averaged $272, and mean rent averaged $170. These estimates include tenants in subsidized housing.

9. Budget Cuts and Rent Control

1. Table 10 differs from the tables in *A Place to Call Home* because I use the 1973 Annual Housing Survey rather than the 1970 Census as my baseline, exclude tenants reporting zero or negative income from my low-income category, and include tenants who paid no cash rent (setting their gross rent equal to their utility bills). These differences do not affect the basic results.

2. For reasons discussed in note 14 of the previous chapter, there are some exceptions to this general rule.

3. Lazere et al., *A Place to Call Home,* p. 30.

4. Paul Leonard, Cushing Dolbeare, and Edward Lazere, *A Place to Call Home: The Crisis in Housing for the Poor* (Washington: Center for Budget and Policy Priorities and Low Income Housing Information Service, 1989), p. 30.

5. House Committee on Ways and Means, *1992 Green Book,* p. 1679. These figures differ slightly from those in Table 10 because tenants who get government subsidies do not always report this fact to the AHS and some subsidies come from sources not covered by the *Green Book.*

6. Measured in constant dollars, total government outlays rose 27 percent between 1980 and 1989, social-security outlays rose 38 percent, defense outlays rose 52 percent, and housing outlays rose 76 percent. See *Statistical Abstract, 1992,* p. 320, and *1992 Green Book,* p. 1681.

7. *The Way Home* (New York City Commission on the Homeless, 1992), p. 87.

8. William Tucker, *The Excluded Americans: Homelessness and Housing Policies* (Washington: Regnery Gateway, 1991).

9. John Quigley, "Does Rent Control Cause Homelessness?" *Journal of Policy Analysis and Management,* 9 (Winter 1990), 89–93.

10. Do Shelters Cause Homelessness?

1. The best exposition of this argument is probably Robert Ellickson, "The Homeless Muddle," *Public Interest* (Spring 1990), 45–60.

2. Bureau of the Census, "Household and Family Characteristics: March 1990 and 1989," *Current Population Reports,* series P-20, no. 447, table A-2.

3. For more details on the New York experience, see Gordon Berlin and William McAllister, "Homelessness," in Henry Aaron and Charles Schultze, eds., *Setting Domestic Priorities: What Can Government Do?* (Washington: Brookings Institution, 1992).

4. Bruce Link, Ezra Susser, Robert Moore, Sharon Schwartz, Elmer Struening, and Ann Stueve, "Reconsidering the Debate about the Size of the Homeless Population," paper delivered at the American Public Health Association, October 1993.

11. Some Partial Solutions

1. Although the homeless often refuse to use shelters, Rossi's 1985–86 survey found that the Chicago homeless expressed a fairly high level of satisfaction with the shelters (*Down and Out in America,* p. 102). Explaining the discrepancy between what the homeless say about shelters and what they do should be a high priority.

2. HUD, "1988 National Survey of Shelters for the Homeless," exhibit 11.

3. Ibid.

4. Ibid., p. 18. Ninety percent of all shelters are privately operated, but privately operated shelters tend to be smaller than publicly operated ones, so private shelters provide only 80 percent of all shelter beds.

5. The figures come from a Yankelovich Clancy Shulman poll for *Time* magazine and CNN, summarized in *The American Enterprise* (September-October 1993), pp. 86–87.

6. Ibid.

7. *1992 Green Book,* p. 943.

8. Ibid., p. 645.

9. The Yankelovich survey found that 92 percent of American adults favored

"spending extra money to provide free day care to allow poor mothers to work or take classes during the day." Yankelovich did not ask the public how much it was willing to spend.

10. For a discussion of single mothers' budgetary needs in Chicago, see Edin and Jencks, "Welfare Reform," in my *Rethinking Social Policy*.

11. Judith Gueron and Edward Pauly, *From Welfare to Work* (New York: Russell Sage, 1991).

12. This estimate is based on the fact that 44.1 percent of all unmarried working-age adults lived in households of which they were neither the head nor the spouse of the head in 1990, while only 22.7 percent of those with 1989 incomes above $30,000 did so. I therefore assumed that an additional 21.4 percent of all unmarried working-age adults would set up their own household if their incomes were above $30,000. The data are from the March 1990 Current Population Survey.